2029

The Post-MAGA Global Financial Market Crash

A Prophetic Novel for a Shaky Planet

Aaron M. Montague
MBA, MDiv, MNLP, MTT, MCHt, MSC

2029

The Post-MAGA Global Financial Market Crash

Published by
Kingdom Publishing, LLC
1350 Blair Drive, Suite F
Odenton, MD 21113

Printed in the United States of America

ISBN: 978-1-967006-35-9 (paperback)
ISBN: 978-1-967006-36-6 (eBook)

This is a work of fiction. Names, characters, places, institutions, brands, events, and incidents either are the product of the author's imagination or are used fictitiously. Any resemblance to actual persons, living or dead, or to actual events is purely coincidental. Real-world institutions, historical events, and public figures are referenced for educational and narrative purposes only. Their inclusion does not imply endorsement.

This book is for spiritual reflection, education, and entertainment. It is not financial, legal, tax, or investment advice. Readers should consult qualified professionals before making any financial decisions.

Unless otherwise noted, Scripture quotations are used in brief, illustrative form and are not intended as exhaustive citations of any particular translation.

Montague Motivational Ministries Press (MX3)
West Philadelphia & Beyond

DEDICATION

To the African Diaspora—
scattered, scarred, brilliant, and still sending money home.

To every grandmother who stretched a dollar, a pound, a cedi, a shilling, a Jamaican dollar, a naira until Heaven took notes.

To the one million "ordinary" believers, hustlers, caregivers, veterans, teachers, coders, and bus drivers who might never be on Forbes, but who are already the largest, quietest investor class on earth.

And to our children and grandchildren,
who deserve to inherit more than trauma and bills—
may you inherit land, ownership, options, and hope.

This is for you.

"The earth is the Lord's, and the fulness thereof;
the world, and they that dwell therein."
— Psalm 24:1 (KJV)

"The crash is not the main character.
The owners are."

ACKNOWLEDGMENTS

I give all glory and honor to God, the Owner of everything, the Author and Finisher of my faith, who keeps letting me play with words, numbers, and nations and still calls me "son."

To my Kingdom Celebration Center (KCC) family, pastored and fathered by Apostle Dr. Antonio and Pastor Dr. Barbara Palmer—thank you for being a living laboratory of faith, courage, and Kingdom economics. You have loved me, stretched me, corrected me, and trusted me with microphones I did not always feel worthy to hold.

To Apostle Zuri and Lady Bria Thorpe, and the emerging leadership generation—you are proof that transition can be holy, orderly, and prophetic all at once.

To my beloved wife, Wanda B. Montague, my life partner and stabilizer of my wildest ideas—thank you for believing in MX3 and WPBS when they were still just scribbles in notebooks and late-night rants.

To my children, grandchildren, and family—natural and spiritual—your lives, your struggles, your victories, and your invoices are in these pages. You are the reason I keep writing, preaching, coaching, and building even when my body says, "Sir, sit down."

To the early readers, clients, and co-laborers in the West Philadelphia Billionaires Society (WPBS) movement—you know who you are. You let me test these crazy-sounding ideas in real time. You sat through sermons that sounded like earnings calls and coaching sessions that felt like altar calls. Thank you for your courage, your critique, and your receipts.

To the financial coaches, cooperative organizers, community land trust builders, Black credit union leaders, CDFI warriors, and quiet remittance senders around the world—you are the hidden heroes in this story. This novel bows in your direction.

And finally, to every reader who dared to pick up a book with "Post-MAGA" and "Global Financial Market Crash" in the title and still found hope, humor, and Holy Ghost inside—thank you. May these pages stir you, not into fear, but into ownership.

AUTHOR'S NOTE TO THE READER

You are holding a strange book on purpose.

This is fiction, but it is not fantasy.

The characters, countries, coins, and crash in these pages are imagined. The emotions, patterns, and systems are not. They are stitched together from real history, real financial crises, real co-ops and credit unions, real massacres, real miracles, real remittance flows, and real church basements where people wrestle with God, with debt, and with destiny.

I am not a prophet of doom. I am a pastor, coach, and veteran who has watched too many "once-in-a-lifetime" crises show up every decade while the same communities keep getting hit hardest.

So I wrote this as a warning, a window, and a weapon:

- A warning that "post-MAGA" does not mean "post-chaos."
- A window into what might happen when AI trading, shadow banking, and digital money meet old-fashioned greed and amnesia.
- A weapon for communities, especially the African Diaspora, to imagine owning more than pain when the next crash comes.

Please hear me clearly:

This book is not telling you what will happen in 2029.

It is inviting you to think differently about what you do between now and whenever your Crash Week arrives.

You will not find investment products in these pages. You will find:

- laundromats,
- land trusts,
- credit unions,
- cooperative businesses,
- remittance flows turned into community capital,
- and a stubborn belief that God did not put us here to be permanent victims of other people's spreadsheets.

Read this slowly. Laugh where you can. Cry where you must. Argue with it. Share it with your book club, your Bible study, your barbershop, your WhatsApp group, your mastermind, your pastor, and your financial advisor.

Then, whatever you do— Don't close the last page and go back to "business as usual."Because if there is one drum this novel keeps beating, it's this:

The crash is not the main character.

The owners are.

And by the grace of God, you might be one of them.

— Aaron M. Montague

PREFACE

(Filed from the Church Basement Investment Committee, West Philadelphia)

Let me say this up front, for the theologians, the traders, and the Twitter prophets. This is fiction. It is prophetic fiction, but still fiction. We are not date-setting the end of the world. We are not predicting which ETF will blow up next. We are not issuing trading signals. If you take investment advice from a book that opens in a church basement and occasionally quotes Scripture alongside crypto, that is between you, your conscience, and your accountant.

What I am doing is this. I am telling a story about a very particular kind of blindness that shows up over and over in history—especially whenever money, power, and human pride get together for brunch.

Economists Carmen Reinhart and Kenneth Rogoff wrote a whole book showing that financial crises are not rare accidents, but recurring patterns stretching across more than eight centuries of global history. They called it This Time Is Different, partly to make fun of our favorite lie: "No, no, this bubble is new and improved. This time it's safe." Another economist, Raghuram Rajan, stood up in 2005 at a fancy conference and asked a very impolite question: Has financial development made the world riskier? He warned that new financial tools could pile up hidden risks and make crises more severe—especially when everybody chased the same short-term incentives.

Polite people nodded. Markets kept partying. Since then, we've seen a procession of "how did that explode?" moments:

- An algorithmic stablecoin ecosystem, TerraUSD and LUNA, that marketed itself as clever, decentralized monetary engineering…until it lost around $40–45 billion in market value in a matter of days in May 2022.

- A crypto exchange, FTX, that rose to global prominence on marketing and trust, then collapsed in November 2022 when an $8-billion hole in customer funds was exposed, leading to bankruptcy and fraud convictions for its founder.
- Wave after wave of bank and non-bank stress—each time followed by confident assurances that "the system is safer now."

Even official voices joined the optimism. In 2017, then–Federal Reserve chair Janet Yellen said she did not expect another financial crisis "in our lifetimes," thanks to post-2008 reforms. It was an expression of confidence, not a prophecy—but history is often unkind to confident statements about crises never returning.

This book lives exactly in that uncomfortable street corner between, "We've learned our lesson," and "We are about to repeat it in a slightly more creative way."

The phrase "Post-MAGA" in the title is not about one politician, one party, or one country. It points to something bigger and more global: a world that has lived through a wave of populist uprisings, culture wars, pandemic shocks, and social-media-fueled outrage cycles—and then decides, a little too quickly, that the "crazy years" are over.

In our story, the post-MAGA era is what happens after people get tired of arguing, without actually fixing the structural problems that produced the arguments in the first place. The crash of 2029 in these pages is not guaranteed to happen on that date, in that way. But the logics behind it—the debt, the shadow banking, the fragile trust, the integration of crypto and traditional finance, the overconfident messaging, the under-regulated corners—those are not imaginary. They are already here, in 2025, breathing quietly in the background.

I am a pastor, a coach, a veteran, and a student of both Scripture and balance sheets. My natural habitat is somewhere between the pulpit and the PowerPoint slide, between West Philadelphia and Wall Street, between altar call and asset allocation. So yes, you will hear Bible language. Yes, you will hear humor—sometimes dark, sometimes just plain silly. Yes, you will hear the voice of a Black man who has watched systems promise fairness and deliver something else.

I write in my own voice because I want this book to feel less like a dry white paper and more like you pulled up a folding chair in the church basement and overheard the Investment Committee talking frankly. No incense. No CNBC graphics. Just people trying to survive, and maybe even build something righteous, in a world that routinely forgets its own lessons.

This is not a manual for day-trading the apocalypse. It is a parable about how societies misprice risk, misread politics, and misunderstand the role of ordinary people in building resilient, community-rooted wealth.

If some of it feels uncomfortably plausible, that's intentional. If some of it makes you laugh out loud at the absurdity of our systems, that's also intentional. If any of it nudges you to think more deeply about how you, your family, your church, and your community prepare for storms—financial and otherwise—that is between you and God.

Now, let's talk about how a world full of very smart people, very powerful institutions, and very sophisticated algorithms could still walk straight into another wall.

Welcome to 2029: The Post-MAGA Global Financial Market Crash.

— Aaron Maxwell Montague

2029

2029 TABLE OF CONTENTS

2029

Introduction

What Do We Mean by "Post-MAGA"?

There's a dangerous moment that shows up after every noisy era. The protests die down. The hashtags change. The angry speeches fade into podcasts nobody listens to anymore. A few scandals get wrapped up with plea deals and documentaries. New faces, new slogans, same unresolved fractures. Then somebody in a nice suit appears on a quiet stage and, in a soothing tone, announces, "We are entering a new chapter of stability." That sentence should come with a warning label.

In this book, "Post-MAGA" does not mean politics suddenly became polite or one particular slogan disappeared from bumper stickers. It means something subtler—and more global—happened:

1. Populism normalized. - The anger that had been shouted from the fringes got folded into mainstream platforms. Trade wars became "strategic industrial policy." Tariffs became "resilience premiums." Capital controls became "financial sovereignty." The emotional energy stayed; the branding changed.
2. Distrust hardened into default. - After disputed elections, pandemic controversies, social-media misinformation, and a steady drip of institutional scandals, more and more people quietly concluded, "Official statistics are massaged. Central banks are political. Rules can flip overnight." That suspicion pushed capital into hard assets, crypto, private markets, and anything that felt outside the reach of traditional gatekeepers.

3. Technocrats tried to fix everything fast. - In reaction to the populist wave, policy elites launched ambitious "rescue" projects: aggressive climate policies, tax reforms, digital currencies, new financial regulations. Some were necessary. Some were overdue. Some were rushed. All of them interacted in messy ways with markets.
4. The plumbing of finance got stranger. Financial activity migrated into the shadows:
   - private credit funds lending where banks used to,
   - money-market-like products promising "cash-plus" returns,
   - DeFi platforms offering algorithmic yield,
   - tokenized "real-world assets" used as collateral in complex chains.

Regulators watched the big banks and sometimes missed the shadows.

None of these trends is imaginary. Economists have been warning for years that financial innovation can expand access to credit and spread risk—and at the same time create new, opaque vulnerabilities. Historical work on crises over centuries shows that periods of optimism, deregulation, and heavy short-term borrowing often precede sudden busts.

Our story takes these real dynamics and pushes them a little further, into a 2029 where:

- sovereign, corporate, and household debts have quietly become unsustainable at higher interest rates,
- shadow banking structures are deeply entangled with crypto and tokenized assets,
- and AI-driven trading systems notice the fragility before human policymakers do.

The "Post-MAGA Global Financial Market Crash" in the title is the moment when all those trends, misperceptions, and incentives collide. It is important to say this clearly, This book is not arguing that a specific crash must happen in 2029. Dates in prophetic fiction are like street signs in a parable.

They give the story shape. The logic behind the crash, however—the way trust erodes, risks migrate, and narratives lull us to sleep—has already shown itself repeatedly in actual crises, from sovereign defaults to bank runs to crypto collapses.

Why Humor in a Book About Crisis? Because without humor, you either break down or tune out. If you lived through the global financial crisis of 2008, the eurozone scare, the COVID crash, meme-stock manias, or the more recent parade of crypto implosions, you know the mix: panic, confusion, and absurdity. A "stablecoin" that isn't stable. An exchange that goes from Super Bowl ads to bankruptcy in a week. Bank CEOs explaining, with a straight face, that nobody could have foreseen risks that had been publicly discussed for years. Humor in this book is not to trivialize loss. It's to expose the ridiculousness of systems that pretend to be all-knowing while constantly rediscovering their own blind spots.

Why Bible in a Book About Global Markets? Because Scripture has been talking about pride, greed, debt, fairness, jubilee, and the treatment of the poor much longer than the International Monetary Fund has. The language may be ancient, but the themes are painfully current.

You will not find proof-texts that say "thou shalt short the S&P 500 in Q2 of 2029." You will find echoes of prophetic warnings about unjust balances, trusting in chariots and horses instead of God, and kingdoms built on exploitation instead of righteousness.

What Is WPBS Doing Here? - The West Philadelphia Billionaires Society (WPBS) in this book is not a hedge fund. It is a community philosophy. It is a group of people who decide they will:

- assume that institutions can fail,
- design their finances for volatility instead of smooth sailing,
- build and own real, local, productive assets,
- and measure wealth not only in dollars, but in dignity, resilience, and shared ownership.

They are not perfect. They are not saints. Some of their investments will make you raise an eyebrow. But they represent a different answer to a world that keeps promising stability and delivering "once-in-a-lifetime" crises every decade.

How This Book Is Structured

- Chapter 1–4: The "Complacent Boom" of 2025–2028
  How the world convinces itself the scary part is over, even as the risks deepen.
- Chapter 5–7: Hairline Cracks in Early 2029
  Minor events that, in hindsight, were major alarms.
- Chapter 8–10: Crash Week
  The 2029 cascade—markets seizing, stablecoins breaking, AI systems front-running panic, and policymakers scrambling.
- Chapter 11–14: WPBS in the Ruins and Beyond
  How a community-driven, barbell-style, faith-rooted approach weathers storms and helps design the next financial order.

No active exercises. No "now close your eyes and visualize your portfolio." Just a story, told in my voice, about what happens when human systems once again believe they are too sophisticated to fail. With that, let's step back a few years from 2029 and see how the stage was set.

2029

Chapter 1

"We Now Return to Our Regularly Scheduled Delusions"

Between 2025 and 2028, the world tried very hard to act normal. The news still had its daily dose of drama—storms, scandals, celebrity feuds—but the financial tone gradually shifted from "everything is on fire" to "we've learned a lot and are stronger for it." Every time a commentator said, "Markets hate uncertainty," I could almost hear the market whisper back, "We love short-term amnesia."

The Comfort of "Never Again"

Back in 2017, long before our story opens, Janet Yellen had expressed strong confidence that, thanks to reforms after 2008, she did not expect another financial crisis "in our lifetimes." The line was meant to reassure people that regulators had tightened rules and banks held more capital.

By the mid-2020s, that sentiment had seeped into the culture. It reappeared in softer forms:

- "We now have better macro-prudential tools."
- "Regulators have learned their lesson."
- "Crypto is risk-managed. Banks are stress-tested. We monitor the system holistically now."

Holistically. That's how you know someone went to a conference. There is nothing wrong with reforms. Many were necessary. But history, as Reinhart and Rogoff documented across eight centuries, has a pattern: after each crisis, the next generation builds a new set of tools, gets comfortable with them, and eventually finds a creative way to blow itself up again. The names change. The leverage feels new. The story is the same.

The Age of Narrative Management

In the post-MAGA period, communications became its own kind of monetary policy. Central banks discovered that phrasing could move markets almost as much as interest rates. A single misplaced adjective in a press conference could erase billions from global equity values. So speeches became carefully scripted, bland to the point of spiritual warfare.

You could watch a two-hour briefing and still not know if rates were going up, down, sideways, or "data-dependent." But you would know that everything was "resilient," "orderly," and "in line with expectations." Corporations followed suit. Every earnings call was a variation on, "We are committed to long-term value creation in a challenging but opportunity-rich macro environment." Translation: Some parts of our business are on life support, but please don't sell the stock. Meanwhile, the real world kept sending small signals that the foundation was less solid than advertised.

Shadow Banking's Quiet Growth Spurt

While regulators focused heavily on big banks—capital buffers, liquidity ratios, stress tests—the action migrated into areas with softer spotlights: private credit, non-bank lenders, money-market-like products, and DeFi platforms. Academic and policy work had already warned that financial innovation can expand access to credit while simultaneously increasing tail risks and amplifying downturns. But shadow structures tend to grow in the spaces where regulation is looser and yield hunger is strongest. Between 2020 and 2028:

- Private credit funds ballooned, offering loans to companies and projects banks no longer wanted on their balance sheets.

- "Cash-plus" products promised slightly higher returns than savings accounts, backed by portfolios few retail investors could truly evaluate.
- Tokenized real-world assets—from real estate to invoices—began circulating as collateral in both traditional and DeFi markets.
- Stablecoins branded themselves as safer, more transparent, or more regulated than the previous generation.

Every previous meltdown—Terra/LUNA's spectacular de-peg in 2022, which wiped out tens of billions in value, or FTX's collapse after misused customer funds were exposed—was treated as a singular morality play: those people were reckless, that pla1tform was shady.

The broader lesson—that leverage and complexity don't disappear, they migrate—was acknowledged in reports, then quietly outvoted by the search for yield.

The AI Boom and the New "This Time Is Different"

At the same time, artificial intelligence became the new electricity, the new internet, the new "whatever metaphor sells the most shares this quarter." Stock indices in several countries became increasingly dominated by a small group of tech and AI-adjacent giants. Their valuations soared to levels reminiscent of late-1990s dot-com peaks, adjusted for the modern inflation of superlatives. Analysts, of course, had convincing explanations:

- "AI will transform productivity across every sector."
- "Winner-take-most dynamics justify premium multiples."
- "We are early in the monetization cycle."

Historically, investors and officials often insist that new technologies justify unprecedented valuations and that long-standing constraints no longer apply—exactly the attitude Reinhart and Rogoff flagged with their title This Time Is Different. Now add AI-driven trading systems that digest headlines, macro data, and order flows at superhuman speed. These systems didn't feel FOMO. They felt statistics. They had been fed data from past booms and busts, including the subprime crisis, the eurozone turmoil, and various emerging-market crashes. Their models looked for patterns in credit growth, asset price momentum, cross-asset correlations, and liquidity conditions.

To humans, 2025–2028 felt like hard-earned calm. To the machines, the numbers quietly began to rhyme with older, less comforting chapters.

The Politics of "Moving On"

Politically, the world was exhausted. After years of sharp slogans, populist rallies, and online conflict, many voters slid into a kind of numb pragmatism. Parties that had once shouted about revolution now promised "predictable stewardship." Politicians who had built careers on disruption rebranded as responsible guardians of order. Some genuinely sought stability. Others simply changed vocabulary. Many post-MAGA leaders tried to straddle two imperatives:

1. Keep some nationalist and populist themes alive—on trade, immigration, and sovereignty—to satisfy their base.
2. Reassure markets and institutions that they were committed to "rules-based order" and "fiscal responsibility."

This balancing act created policy whiplash: sudden tariff announcements, shifting energy rules, digital currency pilots, new climate measures, and occasionally, abrupt subsidies or taxes to calm a given constituency. Each individual policy might have been defensible.

Together, they formed a fog of uncertainty. Investors responded by diversifying not just assets, but jurisdictions:

- Some capital flowed into "onshore safe havens"—government bonds, money markets, major-currency bank deposits.
- Other capital sought "offshore resilience"—crypto assets, foreign real estate, gold, and instruments parked in friendlier legal environments.

What almost nobody did was step back and say, "If everyone is racing for the same exits in a crisis—short-term debt, shadow funds, correlated assets—what happens when we all try to leave at once?"

The Household View: Busy, Tired, and Overexposed

If you zoomed down from the think-tank reports and trading floors into actual households in the late 2020s, you didn't see villains. You saw tired people juggling:

- mortgages or rising rents,
- student loans in countries where those never really got resolved,
- credit cards,
- and whatever was left of their retirement after previous crises.

They were told, repeatedly:

- "Don't worry, the system is safer now."
- "Just stay the course."
- "Volatility is normal."

For many, the only place they felt any control was in the speculative corners:

a crypto portfolio, meme stocks, options trades, a friend's startup, a side hustle chasing algorithmic ad revenue. A lot of that speculative energy came directly out of the scars from earlier crises. When people lose faith that steady work and prudent saving will secure their future, they become more willing to roll the dice. Ironically, that very desperation often becomes raw material for the next bubble.

What the Church Basement Saw

Somewhere in West Philadelphia, a small group kept meeting in a church basement with cheap coffee and expensive opinions. They read some of the same research everyone else did:

- Rajan's warning that financial innovation could expand risk-taking and increase exposure to rare but devastating events.
- Reinhart and Rogoff's evidence that long booms and heavy foreign capital inflows often precede painful reversals.
- Case studies of Terra/LUNA and FTX showing how new platforms could vaporize tens of billions when confidence snapped.

But they also listened to stories:

- The elder who had lived through redlining and knew what it meant when credit dried up on one side of town and flowed freely on another.
- The nurse whose retirement fund had been "rebalanced" into oblivion twice.
- The gig worker whose income rose and fell with algorithms they never saw.

Out of those conversations, a stubborn conviction emerged, "If the global system keeps promising safety and delivering shocks, we should stop treating it like a savior and start treating it like weather." The WPBS mindset formed there—not as a prediction of the exact shape of 2029, but as a refusal to build life on the assumption that central banks, rating agencies, and big platforms would always get it right.

The Seed of the Crash

By the end of 2028, nothing obviously catastrophic had happened. Stock indices, after some wobbles, were near or at new highs in many places. Housing in certain cities felt expensive but "supported by fundamentals." Corporate profits looked solid on the surface, aided by cost-cutting and automation. Governments rolled over their debts, sometimes at higher rates, but always with the promise that growth would catch up. If you only glanced at the headlines, the story was, "We survived the storms. The system held. Onward." But beneath that:

- Debt levels were higher, not lower.
- Shadow banking linkages were denser, not simpler.
- Political trust was thinner, not stronger.
- And AI-driven, high-speed decision-makers were woven into the financial network more tightly than any human could fully map.

The stage was set. All it would take, in 2029, was a small, "contained" event—a mid-size sovereign wobble, a boring fund's redemption halt, a supposedly safe stablecoin slipping its peg—for the comfortable delusions to snap.

In the next chapters, we will walk into that year.

But for now, remember this: The crash of 2029 in this story is not a random thunderbolt. It is the harvest of seeds planted, watered, and fertilized during the "normal" years when everyone wanted to believe the hard part was over. And if history is any guide, that is exactly when we should be paying the most attention.

Chapter 2

Distrust Is the New Default Setting

By the late 2020s, if you wanted to start an argument at a family gathering, all you had to do was say, "Well, I trust ______ ?" Then fill in the blank.

"The government."
"The media."
"The banks."
"The science."
"The blockchain."
"The algorithm."

Didn't matter what you picked. Somebody at that table was going to look at you like you'd just confessed to believing in the Tooth Fairy. It wasn't that people trusted nothing. It was that they trusted nothing unconditionally. They trusted their group chats, their favorite podcaster, their cousin who "does their own research," their anonymous Twitter account with a Greek statue for a profile picture, their preferred economist or pastor or influencer.

But the big systems—the ones that used to carry a sort of default reverence—had lost their aura.

- Government? "Captured."
- Media? "Biased."
- Central banks? "Political."
- Elections? "Rigged, or at least suspicious."
- Courts? "Agenda-driven."
- Big business? "Greedy."

By 2028, distrust wasn't a mood swing. It was the baseline.

The Trust Dashboard Is Flashing Red

If you pulled up a "trust dashboard" for the 2020s, most gauges would be sitting in the yellow or red zone. Long-running polling in the United States found confidence in key institutions—including Congress, the presidency, the Supreme Court, banks, and media—hovering near historic lows, after decades of decline. Global surveys like the Edelman Trust Barometer tracked similar patterns: large segments of the public reported low trust in government and media and expressed skepticism about how innovation and technology were being managed, often seeing them as poorly regulated and influenced by politics and money. You didn't need to read the footnotes to feel it. You could hear it:

At the barbershop - "They say inflation is cooling. My grocery bill did not get that memo."

In the church lobby - "The experts said they had it under control last time, too."

On social media - "Fact-checkers are just censors with better branding."

One Harvard youth poll in the mid-2020s found that less than one in five young Americans trusted the federal government to "do the right thing most or all of the time," with faith in Congress even lower. If the elders were jaded, the kids were tired before they even got started. And it wasn't just one side of the aisle. Polling showed that trust in government swung dramatically depending on whether your preferred party held power, while overall confidence in institutions like courts fell sharply across the spectrum. We weren't in an age of "trust but verify." We had moved into "assume it's spin until proven otherwise."

Infodemic Hangover

Then came the pandemic—and, more importantly for our story, the pandemic of information about the pandemic. The World Health Organization coined a term for it: infodemic—too much information, including false or misleading content, flooding digital and physical environments, fueling confusion, mistrust, and harmful behavior. Researchers later documented how COVID-19 misinformation and disinformation spread through social media platforms at high speed, mixing accurate guidance with conspiracy theories, rumors, and politicized narratives.

People watched health guidance change over time as experts learned more about the virus. That's how science works—new data, updated recommendations. But in an already suspicious environment, those changes looked, to many eyes, like proof that someone had been lying all along. By the time the worst of the pandemic passed, millions had internalized a simple, corrosive rule, "If the official story changes, it means it was fake from the start." It didn't matter that evolving guidance is normal in complex crises.

The emotional verdict was in.

When the next big topic came along—climate policies, digital currencies, geopolitical conflicts, election results—large chunks of the public treated every official statement as a potential psy-op. The old model was: authority speaks, we mostly accept. The new model was: authority speaks, we screenshot, dissect, and meme it to death.

Elections Everyone Lost

Elections were supposed to be the great legitimacy machine: we vote, someone wins, someone loses, the system moves on. Instead, they became another trust minefield. Around the world, analysts documented disinformation campaigns targeting elections and political crises, often involving both domestic and foreign actors.

These efforts didn't always change outcomes—but they did undermine confidence in the integrity of the process.

In the United States, a 2024 post-election study highlighted growing concerns about trust in government messaging and democratic institutions. Combine that with years of high-profile claims about "stolen" or "rigged" elections, investigations, court cases, and counter-claims, and many citizens reached a depressing conclusion, "Elections are about power, not truth. My side only believes the results when we win."

Media trust played its own role. Research heading into the 2020 election showed Republicans and Democrats inhabiting almost opposite news environments, each side trusting outlets the other side distrusted. That polarization didn't disappear in the years that followed—it evolved, diversified, went onto new platforms, but the basic divide remained. In that atmosphere, every result had at least three narratives:

1. The official count.
2. The losing side's explanation.
3. A half-dozen viral alternative theories.

The math might be straightforward. The meaning was up for grabs.

When the Banking App Turns Into a Horror Movie

If you really want to stress-test trust, touch people's money. In March 2023, Silicon Valley Bank collapsed after a rapid bank run, becoming the largest U.S. bank failure since the 2008 crisis and the second-largest bank failure in U.S. history. The mechanics were complicated enough for textbooks:

- SVB had loaded up on long-term securities when rates were low.
- When rates rose sharply, the market value of those holdings fell.
- Losses crystallized when the bank sold assets, triggering concerns.
- Depositors, many of them tech firms and startups, rushed to pull funds.Regulators intervened, closed the bank, and arranged backstops for depositors.

Official statements emphasized that the broader system was sound, that this was a contained failure driven by poor risk management and concentrated deposit bases. But to ordinary people, the storyline was simpler and more alarming. One day, a well-known bank app on your phone works. The next day, it is on the news as a failure. That kind of whiplash doesn't make you a technical expert in interest-rate risk. It makes you wonder what else you're not being told.

SVB wasn't alone. Other regional banks showed stress that year. Regulators later billed larger institutions with special assessments to cover costs, leading to lawsuits from banks arguing they were overcharged for the clean-up.

Meanwhile, former executives from another failed bank launched a new blockchain-based institution built on the promise of fully backed deposits, no lending, and real-time transparency—a direct response to fears about traditional models. To the average depositor, the message from all sides amounted to:

- "Trust us, we've got this."
- "Also, we are suing each other about who should pay for who didn't have this."
- "And here's a new bank that promises to be better than all the others."

You don't need a PhD in finance to see why people start keeping a little extra cash under the mattress and a little extra Bitcoin in a cold wallet.

Trust as a Luxury Good

By the time our story edges toward 2029, trusting major institutions felt like a luxury—something you could afford if you had buffers, connections, and options. If you were doing well, you might say, "Sure, the system is imperfect, but it works well enough for me."

If you were living closer to the edge, you were more likely to say, "The system works mostly for them. I'm just trying not to get run over." And if you were young, looking at climate risks, housing prices, student loans, and a job market increasingly shaped by AI, you might say, "They had their chance. Look where we are." Trust became heavily segmented:

- Some still trusted national institutions but distrusted global ones.
- Some trusted local organizations but not national politics.
- Some trusted markets but not regulators.
- Some trusted alternative platforms and influencers more than any formal authority.

Surveys reflected this fragmentation. Analysis of global trust trends found that developed democracies often showed lower trust in institutions than some developing countries, with people citing concerns about inequality, political polarization, and captured elites. In the U.S., trust in courts slid to record lows, with especially sharp drops among groups who felt the justice system had become an openly political battlefield.

The phrase "rule of law" still appeared in speeches. The lived experience told a different story. Distrust as an Investment Strategy.

Here's where our narrative connects directly to money. When distrust becomes default, people don't just complain; they rearrange their portfolios—formally and informally.

On the informal side:

- Folks kept larger emergency cash reserves.
- They invested more in family networks—helping siblings, adult children, and parents in ways that substituted for fraying public systems.
- They favored side hustles, gig work, and entrepreneurial experiments over trusting a single employer.

On the formal side:

- Wealthier and more sophisticated investors increased exposure to hard assets—energy, commodities, farmland, infrastructure—on the theory that these would hold value even if financial promises wobbled.
- Others moved into crypto and digital assets, not because they expected a smooth ride, but because they preferred math-based rules, even volatile ones, over policymaker discretion.
- Many sought jurisdictional diversification, using foreign accounts, multi-currency holdings, and cross-border structures to hedge against any one government's decisions.

Academic and policy analysis started to pay more attention to what some called "geo-economic fragmentation": capital, data, and supply chains reorganizing along political lines, as trust in a single integrated global order eroded. In a quiet way, distrust itself became an investment thesis, "Assume they will mismanage. Assume rules will change mid-game. Own what survives chaos." Now, here's the twist. That mindset can lead to two very different paths:

1. Predatory opportunism—betting on chaos and rooting for collapse, because you stand to gain.
2. Resilient stewardship—accepting that storms come, preparing wisely, and using your relative strength to protect and rebuild, not exploit.

The difference between those paths is moral, not mathematical.

The WPBS View: Weather, Not Religion

In our West Philadelphia church basement, we didn't treat global finance as a religion—something to worship—or as a cartoon villain—something to simply hate. We treated it like weather:

- You can't control it by yelling at the clouds.
- You can't predict it perfectly.
- But you can pay attention, build better roofs, and stop pretending a hurricane is "unexpected" when the radar has been loud for days.

When we looked at the trust landscape, we didn't just see anger. We saw patterns:

- Long-term data showing declining confidence in big institutions.
- Studies documenting the infodemic and the way misinformation undermined public health and political trust.
- Bank failures that arrived suddenly for the public but had been foreshadowed in risk metrics and supervisory reports.
- Youth polls showing a generation already disillusioned with government.

We concluded three things:

1. Trust is precious and perishable.
   Once squandered, you don't get it back with a press release.
2. Blind faith and total cynicism are both dangerous.
   Blind faith makes you easy to exploit. Total cynicism makes you easy to paralyze.
3. Communities need their own resilience plans.
   You can't outsource your survival to institutions that have already shown you their limitations.

So, while the world argued online about whether to "trust the system" or "burn it all down," WPBS quietly worked on a third option, "We will be courteous to the system, cooperative where we can, but we will not build our entire future on the assumption that it will behave." That meant organizing around:

- Local ownership of essential services where possible.
- Diversified savings and investments, not just in Wall Street tickers but in Main Street businesses.
- Liquid reserves, so folks didn't have to dump assets at the worst time.
- Skills and relationships, not just financial instruments.

We weren't against innovation, or against global markets, or against technology. We were against unquestioned dependence.

In a world where distrust had become the default setting, we wanted to practice something more nuanced:

"We trust God absolutely.

We trust people conditionally.

We trust systems provisionally.

And we keep our eyes open."

The Cost of Living in "Nothing Is Real"

Of course, there was a downside to permanent suspicion. You can't build a functioning society if everyone believes every institution is lying all the time. That way lies conspiracy fever, paralysis, and an inability to cooperate even when cooperation is plainly in everyone's interest. We saw some of that, too:

- Public health campaigns undermined by misinformation and distrust.
- Climate conversations turning into tribal identity tests rather than problem-solving.
- Courts and legal processes treated as partisan weapons, eroding respect for the rule of law.
- People so overwhelmed by conflicting narratives that they opted out of engagement altogether.

Distrust can protect you from naïveté. It can also starve you of healthy dependence—on good institutions, on competent professionals, on shared facts.

In financial markets, permanent skepticism can keep you from getting scammed. It can also keep you sitting in cash until inflation quietly picks your pocket. So the real challenge—moral and practical—was not simply to distrust more. It was to discern better.

Our coming crash in 2029 will expose the difference:

- Some actors will profit from distrust by designing products that feed fear and complexity.
- Others will acknowledge distrust, design for resilience, and then show up when neighbors are hurting.

One group will say, "I told you so." The other will say, "We planned for this. Let's work."By the end of 2028, the world's trust muscles were badly strained. People no longer believed the old promises—but they hadn't yet built new, credible structures to replace them. That gap between crumbling faith and unready alternatives was one of the quiet fault lines under the 2029 crash.

In the next chapter, we'll look at how the financial story "This time is definitely different" layered itself on top of this distrust—and why, once again, those four words turned out to be very expensive.

2029

Chapter 3

"This Time Is Definitely Different"

There are four very expensive words in finance: "This time is different." They are tattooed on the ghost of every bubble that ever burst. They floated over tulip mania in 17th-century Holland. They hummed through railroad manias and South Sea schemes. They danced over the dot-com bubble of the late 1990s, when a Federal Reserve chair stepped up to a podium in December 1996 and asked, with professorial caution, whether markets were showing signs of "irrational exuberance." Investors heard the warning… and replied, "Probably. But have you seen our new valuation model?"

Fast-forward a quarter century. The phrase "irrational exuberance" lives on in financial history, in Robert Shiller's book of the same name, and in countless think pieces about bubbles. Yet the basic dance has not changed:

1. A transformative technology appears.
2. Early successes make people rich.
3. Valuations climb beyond what traditional models can justify.
4. Pundits split into "bubble!" and "new paradigm!" camps.
5. The story ends with a boom, a crash, and a lot of "in hindsight" wisdom.

By the late 2020s, that old script was back on stage—this time wearing an AI hoodie.

AI: Miracle, Mirage, or Both?

Let's be clear: artificial intelligence was not fake. Real systems wrote code, drafted documents, reviewed scans, translated languages, answered customer queries, analyzed medical images, and optimized logistics. Whole sectors reorganized around the promise of AI-driven productivity. Companies that built chips, cloud infrastructure, and large-scale models printed revenue and free cash flow that the dot-com dreamers of 1999 could only fantasize about.

But in markets, truth plus excitement often turns into truth plus leverage plus story, which is how you get bubbles. Analysts pointed out that the so-called "Magnificent Seven"—Nvidia, Microsoft, Alphabet, Amazon, Meta, Tesla, and Apple—had grown to represent around 30% of the entire S&P 500's market capitalization, much of it on the back of AI enthusiasm. Some traded at forward price-to-earnings ratios above 50 or 70, levels associated with the dot-com era.

One research note observed that certain companies saw their valuation jump simply by mentioning "AI" in their strategy, even when actual AI revenue was modest.

If you had lived through 1999, where companies could add ".com" to their name and double their stock price, this felt familiar—just with better graphics and more GPUs.

At the same time, some large asset managers and banks argued that, unlike the dot-com bubble, today's tech and AI leaders were highly profitable, with strong balance sheets and real cash flows. One analysis noted that, at the peak of the dot-com era, top tech leaders traded around 70 times forward earnings, while major AI hyperscalers in the mid-2020s traded closer to 25–26 times forward earnings—elevated, but not as extreme. So which was it?

- A bubble set to pop disastrously?
- A justified repricing of companies that would dominate the next several decades?
- Or something in between: a real revolution with a very excitable fan club?

Different observers picked different narratives:

- Some commentators and strategists began writing about an "AI valuation bubble," pointing to AI-related gains concentrated in a small group of stocks, lofty multiples, and parallels to the late 1990s.
- Others pushed back, claiming that strong earnings growth, infrastructure investment, and relatively lower leverage compared to 1999 meant we were "nowhere near" those extremes.

If you were looking for certainty, you picked the wrong decade.

The Gold Rush and the Power Bill

One CEO compared the AI excitement to a gold rush: the real money, she argued, might be less in the "miners" (AI applications) and more in the companies selling shovels—in this case, chips, networking gear, and data centers. Infrastructure spending surged:

- Chipmakers ramped production of advanced GPUs.
- Cloud giants poured billions into data centers.
- Telecom and networking firms upgraded their equipment to handle AI-driven traffic.
- Smaller "neo-cloud" firms leased capacity, filled it with GPU clusters, and rented it out to AI startups.

Analysts projected that global data center capacity could increase several-fold by the 2030s, requiring trillions of dollars in investment. But commentaries also warned that this expansion relied heavily on cheap financing and long-dated leases with tenants whose credit quality was not always stellar. One analysis estimated that to justify projected AI infrastructure spending, the industry might need to generate trillions of dollars in additional annual revenue by 2030—

comparable to a sizable fraction of U.S. GDP—and warned that those targets might be optimistic. In other words:

- The technology was real.
- The use cases were real.
- The power bill and capex were very real.

The question was whether the cash flows would arrive fast enough, and in large enough volume, to match the story. If they did, the 2020s AI boom would be remembered as the early innings of a world-changing transformation. If they didn't, well… people would dust off the word "bubble" again, maybe with an AI-generated font.

Old Ghosts, New Clothes

The dot-com bust of 2000–2002 left scar tissue on anyone who had watched the Nasdaq rocket up nearly 90% in 1999 and then fall roughly 78% from peak to trough over the next few years. Back then:

- Companies went public with little more than a website, a Super Bowl ad, and a plan to "monetize eyeballs."
- Valuations were justified with new metrics—"price per click," "price per pageview"—because traditional measures like earnings and free cash flow were scarce.
- When the tide went out, it exposed flimsy business models, weak balance sheets, and unrealistic assumptions.

As 2025 rolled into 2028, commentators started writing familiar headlines:

- "Is This 1996 or 1999?"—asking whether the current tech rally was in its early or late bubble phase.
- "Are AI Stocks in a Bubble?"—debating whether concentrated gains and high multiples were sustainable.
- "AI Valuation Bubble Getting Silly"—noting that some companies with minimal AI revenue were still enjoying AI-size valuations.

Historical perspective pieces pointed out that, around the turn of the millennium, tech's share of the S&P 500 roughly doubled in under two years, from about 23% to nearly 47%. By contrast, in the mid-2020s, tech and AI-heavy firms reached similar or greater shares of major indices, but over a longer period, with stronger earnings behind them—suggesting important differences as well as similarities. Even central bankers and regulators, who usually speak in measured tones, began referencing AI-related valuations as a potential source of risk, while investors who had once warned about housing or credit bubbles started writing memos about AI-driven exuberance and the possibility of a hard landing when expectations met reality. It would have been comforting if everyone agreed on one clean narrative: "Yes, it's a bubble. Avoid it." or "No, it's justified. Relax."

Instead, the truth sat uncomfortably between them, like a guest at Thanksgiving who belongs to both sides of the family.

The Story Everyone Needed to Believe

Here's the thing about "this time is different" stories: they're not only about money. They're about meaning. For many countries in the late 2020s, AI was not just a sector. It was a national storyline:

- "AI will restore our productivity growth."
- "AI will secure our strategic advantage over rival powers."
- "AI will offset demographic decline and aging populations."
- "AI will rescue our stock market and our pension funds."

A commentary in late 2025, for example, highlighted how AI spending in the United States had become a crucial support for economic growth, with some analysts suggesting that, without it, the economy might already be in recession—and warning that the boom could not continue forever at its current pace. Another report described how the AI rally had pushed broad market indexes to record highs, only to see enthusiasm falter when investors began questioning whether capital expenditures on AI would translate into sustainable profits.

In that context, doubting the AI story felt almost unpatriotic. It wasn't just a financial thesis; it was a promise that the future could still be bigger than the past. That made it harder, emotionally and politically, to ask boring but necessary questions:

- "What if the revenue projections are wrong?"
- "What if a handful of firms capture most of the gains, leaving everyone else with the bill?"
- "What if the infrastructure is overbuilt or financed on terms that don't survive higher interest rates?"
- "What happens to workers displaced by automation if the expected growth doesn't arrive?"

Those questions didn't disappear. They just moved into quieter corners—risk reports, academic journals, footnotes, late-night memos. In the public square, the louder message was: "Yes, there are risks, but the upside is too big to ignore. And anyway, we can always manage the fallout." Sound familiar?

The Algorithms Take Notes

AI wasn't just the subject of the bubble story; it was also among its narrators. Large investment firms deployed AI models to analyze markets, detect patterns, and optimize portfolios. Quantitative funds used machine learning to parse news headlines, earnings transcripts, and social-media chatter in real time. High-frequency traders used increasingly sophisticated algorithms to make micro-second decisions. Some research and commentary began to ask whether these AI-enhanced, automated strategies could amplify volatility—

especially if they were trained on historical episodes where rapid selling cascaded into full-blown crashes. Think about the irony:

- AI systems learned from past bubbles and busts,
- then deployed that knowledge to trade assets whose value partly depended on expectations about AI.

The feedback loop was tight:

1. AI hype drove AI company valuations.
2. AI trading models chased momentum in AI stocks.
3. Risk models, also aided by AI, gradually grew comfortable with higher valuations.
4. Until something—earnings, regulation, interest rates, a scandal—triggered a reassessment.

In our story, those same AI systems will later play a starring role in Crash Week 2029, when they notice a pattern faster than most humans and start selling into a market still listening to soothing human voices. But the seeds of that moment were sown here, in the mid-2020s, when we invited AI both to power the economy and to interpret it.

The WPBS Side-Eye

While the world debated whether "AI is the new electricity" or "AI is the new tulip," the WPBS crew watched with a mixture of respect, curiosity, and holy skepticism. From our church basement vantage point, a few things stood out:

1. **Real Productivity, Real Disruption**
   We knew AI could genuinely boost productivity. It could also wipe out jobs, compress wages, and concentrate power in the hands of companies and governments with the best models and most data. That tension between innovation and inequality was not hypothetical; it was

already on the ground in automation, gig work, and algorithmic management.

2. **Concentration Risk**
   When seven companies make up nearly a third of a major index, you don't need a PhD to know you're not as diversified as the brochure suggests.
3. **Infrastructure Overhang**
   Massive data center build-outs financed with debt and long-term contracts looked profitable in bullish scenarios, but very fragile if rates stayed high or demand under-delivered.
4. **Narrative Addiction**
   Policymakers, executives, and investors all needed the AI story to be true—economically, politically, emotionally. That made it harder to hear cautionary voices, even when they came from experienced investors and sober analysts.

So WPBS made a simple decision: "We will respect AI. We will use AI. But we will not worship AI, and we will not bet our whole future on AI valuations staying pretty."

In practical terms, that meant:

- Owning infrastructure and essentials likely to be needed whether AI soared or stumbled: energy, water, food systems, local housing, community businesses.
- Treating direct AI-related investments as speculative satellites, not the core of the portfolio.
- Preparing for scenarios where AI increased inequality and volatility—and where backlash, regulation, or simple disappointment could cause sharp repricings.

In sermons and strategy sessions, we sometimes joked: "If the robots take all the jobs, somebody still has to own the building, the land, and the power company. Let's talk about that." Humor softened the edge, but the conviction underneath was firm.

"Different" Doesn't Mean "Safe"

By 2028, the official line went something like this:

- "Yes, tech and AI valuations are elevated, but earnings are strong."
- "Yes, there are bubble concerns, but this is not 1999."
- "Yes, AI spending is enormous, but it underpins growth and competitiveness."

All of that might have been true. But here is the lesson history keeps teaching and we keep forgetting: Not being exactly like the last bubble doesn't mean you're not in a bubble. Different leverage structures, different policy regimes, different technologies—those change the details of how a crash unfolds. They do not repeal the basic physics:

- When expectations outrun cash flows,
- when concentration meets complacency,
- when stories outrun balance sheets,
- when everyone leans to the same side of the boat…

…you don't need the crisis to look like 1999 or 2008 for it to hurt like 1999 or 2008.

"This time is different" might be technically true—different seeds, different soil, different weather. But crops of disappointment can still grow there.

By the end of the "Complacent Boom," the AI narrative had fused with the post-MAGA desire for stability and victory:

- "We survived the populist storms."

- "We survived the pandemic."
- "Now we ride the AI wave into a prosperous, data-driven future."

The stage was set for 2029:

- Fragile trust (Chapter 2).
- Complex, opaque financial plumbing (Chapter 1).
- A technology boom that was both real and over-narrated (this chapter).

All it needed was a spark—a small, "contained," technical problem that exposed how much of the global financial story had been resting on stories rather than solid ground.

In the next chapter, we'll watch that spark land—in a place so boring, so allegedly safe, that almost no one saw it as the match it really was.

Chapter 4

The Quiet Explosion in the Shadows

If the AI boom was the loud, flashy teenager of the 2020s—all GPUs and grand pronouncements—shadow banking was the quiet uncle in the corner you really should've been watching. On paper, we called it "non-bank financial intermediation" (NBFI) because "shadow banking" sounds like a Marvel villain. But the idea was simple: Any place where credit, maturity transformation, and leverage happen outside of regular banks. That includes:

- money market funds
- hedge funds
- open-ended bond funds and ETFs
- private credit funds
- finance companies and securitization vehicles
- broker-dealers and securities lenders

In other words, a whole other financial system, stitched together with contracts and confidence, sitting next to the banking system like a twin that decided not to get a banking license. And by the 2020s, the twin had been hitting the gym.

Almost Half the World's Finance, Off to the Side

By the mid-2020s, global watchdogs were sounding very polite but very serious alarms. A 2025 Congressional Research Service report summarized that non-bank financial intermediaries collectively held almost half of global financial assets, with the Financial Stability Board (FSB) estimating broad NBFI assets rising from about $67 trillion in 2004 to roughly $238 trillion by 2023. In the United States alone, that same analysis noted that:

- Total financial assets at U.S. NBFIs reached about $85.7 trillion in 2023,
- compared to about $31.1 trillion at banks—roughly 313% of U.S. GDP vs. 114% for banks.

Let that sink in for a second. The world kept saying "the banks are safer now."Meanwhile, a much larger ecosystem of non-banks had grown up around them like ivy on a wall. International bodies weren't asleep. The FSB's 2023 Global Monitoring Report on NBFI and the IMF's 2023 Global Financial Stability Report both highlighted vulnerabilities in NBFIs linked to leverage, liquidity mismatch, and interconnectedness with core markets—especially in open-ended investment funds and money-like instruments. By 2025, the FSB was going further, urging governments to address non-bank risks and recommending tools like leverage limits and better monitoring of "runnable" structures—structures where investors can rush for the exits and cause fire sales. But here's the problem: When you have hundreds of trillions of dollars sitting in complex, fragmented, globally scattered vehicles… getting your arms around that risk is like trying to hug fog.

The Dash for Cash: A Trailer for the Main Feature

The 2029 crash in this book doesn't come out of nowhere. We already had a preview screening in March 2020. When COVID fears hit markets that month, investors around the world went into what the New York Fed later called a "global dash for cash"—selling even safe assets like government bonds to raise liquidity. It was like watching people raid the bottled water aisle and the fire hydrants at the same time. Here's what that episode revealed:

- Prime money market funds—sold as conservative cash parking lots—faced heavy redemptions and had to be backstopped, again.
- Open-ended bond funds let investors redeem daily, even when the underlying bonds were illiquid, creating incentives to run before prices fully reflected bad news.
- Dealer balance sheets and repo markets got strained, forcing central banks to step in with massive interventions just to keep government bond markets functioning.

A BIS study documented how institutional prime money market funds faced twenty straight days of outflows, while an FSB review flagged how some open-ended funds created "first-mover advantage" dynamics—redeem early, or risk being stuck with losses. Regulators looked at all this and said, in essence: "Interesting. Concerning. We should definitely do more about that soon." Then markets recovered, asset prices soared, and the urgency faded—at least in the political imagination. The plumbing, however, had been exposed:

- Non-banks could amplify stress, not just absorb it.
- Central banks were becoming lenders of last resort to markets, not just to banks.
- Every time they stepped in, markets learned a quiet lesson:

  "If it gets bad enough, Daddy will fix it."

That's not exactly the incentive you want in a world already hooked on leverage.

Private Credit: Banks in Everything but Name

If you want to see how activity migrates into the shadows, look at private credit. Instead of banks making loans and keeping them, you had funds and vehicles—often backed by institutional investors—

making loans directly to companies, often with fewer disclosure requirements and less public trading.

A 2025 Federal Reserve note estimated that in the U.S., the private credit market had grown in real terms from about $46 billion in 2000 to roughly $1 trillion by 2023, with growth accelerating after 2019. By the mid-2020s:

- S&P and other analysts were warning that private credit's rapid growth, opacity, and looming maturity cliffs (peaking around 2028) could pose systemic risk if conditions turned.
- The Financial Stability Board and the G20's watchdog explicitly flagged private credit markets as emerging vulnerabilities that needed close monitoring and better data.
- Bank of America research called private credit "the lowest-quality asset class in the leveraged finance landscape" and warned of fragility even as the sector swelled to around $3 trillion globally by early 2025.

At the same time, defenders of private credit argued that:

- Funds were less leveraged than banks,
- Deals often had tighter covenants than some syndicated loans,
- And the market provided valuable financing where banks had pulled back after 2008.

In other words, even among experts, the jury was still out:

- Is private credit a pressure valve, making the system safer by spreading risk?
- Or a pressure cooker, loading up opaque obligations that could blow in a downturn?

Either way, by late 2020s, the cooks had turned the heat up. And it wasn't just stand-alone funds anymore. A 2025 Fed analysis documented how banks themselves were lending tens of billions to private credit vehicles through revolving lines and term loans—creating tight interconnections between the regulated and unregulated worlds. So if something went wrong in private credit, you couldn't just say, "Oh, that's over there." "Over there" had borrowing facilities at your friendly neighborhood bank.

Tokenization: Putting the Shadow on Chain

While all this was happening, another quiet revolution was underway: tokenization of real-world assets. In theory, it was simple: Take a real-world thing—Treasury bills, real estate, invoices, credit claims—represent it as a digital token on a blockchain, and now it can move faster, trade 24/7, and be sliced into tiny pieces.

By 2024–2025, reports from crypto research firms and DeFi analytics showed that tokenized real-world assets (excluding stablecoins) had grown into a multi-billion-dollar market, with estimates around $15.2 billion by late 2024 and over $24 billion by mid-2025, roughly an 85% year-over-year increase.

Common categories included:

- tokenized U.S. Treasuries and securities,
- on-chain private credit claims,
- tokenized real estate and receivables,
- even more exotic assets like carbon credits and fine art.

International bodies noticed. The FSB's 2024 report on the financial stability implications of tokenisation warned that:

- Any type of existing asset can, in principle, be tokenised,
- Tokenisation can increase interconnectedness between traditional finance and DeFi,

- And poorly designed tokenised structures could amplify runs and fire-sale dynamics if widely adopted.

You know what that sounds like? Shadow banking… with better UX. Now your "safe, boring" real-world asset could be:

- rehypothecated across multiple DeFi platforms,
- pledged as collateral for leveraged bets,
- and wrapped in layers of smart contracts that most investors never read—all while regulators were still arguing about which agency should be in charge.

To be fair, some tokenisation efforts were cautious, tightly regulated, and institution-only. Others… not so much. But from a systemic point of view, the direction of travel was clear:

- More credit intermediation outside banks,
- More market-based funding with daily liquidity promises,
- More tokenised claims sitting in both TradFi and DeFi,
- More stablecoins linking digital money to underlying assets, growing fast enough that the FSB and G20 kept issuing politely urgent letters about "significant gaps" in global crypto rules and the need for stablecoin oversight.

All of that added up to a simple truth: By the late 2020s, the "shadow" in shadow banking wasn't dark; it was everywhere, in plain sight, but too complex to see clearly.

Runnable Promises Everywhere

One of the most worrying patterns, according to IMF and FSB work, was the spread of "runnable" structures—places where investors can demand their money back quickly, even when the underlying assets are not so quick.

Examples:

- Money market funds promising stable values but holding instruments that can move.
- Open-ended bond funds letting you redeem daily while holding thinly traded debt.
- Stablecoins offering instant on-chain redemption for supposedly safe reserves.
- Tokenised credit pools letting investors exit on short notice while the loans themselves are long-term and illiquid.

Regulators had already seen how this movie ends:

- In 2008, money market funds "broke the buck" and required extraordinary support.
- In 2020, the dash for cash hit MMFs and bond funds again, prompting more central bank interventions.

By 2025, U.S. securities regulators were openly warning that, left unchecked, run-prone features in money market funds could undermine financial stability in future stress events, pointing directly back to 2008 and March 2020 as cautionary tales.

At the same time, a U.S. CRS report laid out how NBFI entities—from hedge funds to bond ETFs to MMFs—could transmit shocks through:

- leverage,
- liquidity mismatch,
- interconnectedness with banks,
- and concentrated exposures to similar assets.

Think of it like this:

- Banks are built with sprinkler systems, fire doors, and fire drills (capital requirements, stress tests, resolution plans).

- The shadow system is a massive warehouse district where some buildings have sprinklers, some have candles, some have illegal wiring, and nobody's really sure who insures what.

Most days, nothing bad happens. On the day it does, everybody finds out how close the buildings are.

The Boiling-Frog Problem

Why didn't we fix this? Partly because…

- Shadow banking supports growth. It provides credit where banks won't: small businesses, leveraged buyouts, emerging markets, niche asset classes.
- Investors love yield. Low rates in the 2010s and early 2020s pushed pensions, insurers, and individuals into anything offering a bit more return.
- Regulation is slow. Each step—consultation, comment period, implementation—takes years. Markets evolve faster than working groups.
- Lobbying is loud. Every time regulators propose tougher rules on non-banks, someone writes a 40-page comment letter explaining that innovation will die, jobs will vanish, and the sky will fall.

So what we got was a compromise:

- Reports.
- Recommendations.
- Partial reforms.
- Pilot stress tests (like the Bank of England's new private-markets stress exercise).

All helpful. All incremental. All running behind the speed of innovation, global capital flows, and clever structuring.

Meanwhile, the FSB's own data showed the NBFI sector expanding by about 130% between 2009 and 2023, ending up near half of global financial assets and deeply entwined with government bond markets and derivatives.So you had:

- Bigger shadows,
- More leverage,
- More "runnable" structures,
- And more tokenised bridges between TradFi and DeFi…

…in a world where trust was already frayed (Chapter 2), and valuations were stretched by the AI story (Chapter 3).

WPBS: Reading the Footnotes

In the church basement, we didn't have access to secret data. We had:

- Public reports from the FSB and IMF,
- Congressional research summaries,
- BIS working papers,
- SEC speeches,
- And a healthy suspicion whenever someone said "contained."

We noticed a few themes:

1. **Size vs. Visibility**
   The non-bank sector was huge, but poorly mapped. When official reports talk about "data gaps" and "limited transparency," that's polite technocrat language for "we don't fully know where all the risk is."
2. **Banks and Shadows Are Intertwined**
   Banks lent to NBFIs, relied on them for funding, and traded with them in derivatives and repo. You couldn't ring-fence the shadows. They were sitting on the same couch as the banks, sharing snacks.

3. **Regulators Were Worried Enough to Say It Out Loud**
   When a G20 watchdog repeatedly tells leaders that private credit and stablecoins need close monitoring, that NBFI leverage requires direct limits, and that crypto rules have "significant gaps," you should hear the subtext:

"We see smoke. We're not sure exactly where the fire is. Please don't cut the fire department's budget."

So, WPBS formed a simple theology of the shadows: "If they can't see it clearly,

we will not anchor our future to it." We did not swear off all market investing. But we:

- Treated shadow-linked exposures as fragile, not foundational.
- Assumed any yield premium might be payment for illiquidity and complexity, not a free lunch.
- Prioritized assets and ventures we could touch, visit, and understand—local businesses, real property, essential services—over fancy vehicles that needed 80-page offering memoranda and three acronyms just to explain the strategy.

We weren't trying to out-trade Wall Street. We were trying to not be the last ones holding the bag when Wall Street and its shadow cousins had another family fight.

A Fuse, Not Just Background Noise

By the time 2029 arrives in this story, shadow banking isn't just background texture. It's part of the fuse.

- Private credit structures heavily exposed to floating-rate borrowers and weakening covenants start to creak as higher-for-longer rates bite.
- Tokenised credit pools and stablecoins, tightly woven into on- and off-chain collateral chains, transmit stress in surprising directions.
- Liquidity mismatches in open-ended funds, MMFs, and some tokenised vehicles invite runs at the first sign of serious trouble.
- Banks, who thought they offloaded risk to non-banks, discover they are on the hook through credit lines, derivatives, and reputational pressure.

None of that guarantees the exact shape of the 2029 crash. But all of it makes the system more brittle, more complex, and more sensitive to a shock that might, in a simpler world, have been absorbable. In other words: The shadows don't cause every storm.

But they make every storm more interesting… in the worst way.

In the next chapter, we'll watch the spark land: Not in a glamorous AI stock, not in a dramatic bank run, but in something so supposedly safe and boring that, at first, almost nobody notices… Until the shadows start to move.

2029

Chapter 5

When a "Small Country" Sneezed

If you've ever watched the news anchors on a slow financial day, you know they love a certain sentence: "Markets are shrugging off concerns about a small country..." Beloved, that sentence should make the hair on the back of your neck stand up. Because what the world calls "a small country" is usually somebody's whole universe—millions of people, real families, real lives. And in modern finance, so-called small countries are often welded into the global machine in ways the commentators do not fully appreciate.

The first real crack of 2029 didn't come from a G7 summit, an AI mega-cap earnings miss, or a Wall Street titan. It came from a place most folks could barely find on a map without zooming in twice. We'll call it San Aurelio. Mid-sized emerging economy. Not poor enough to feature in late-night charity ads, not rich enough to host Davos. A country that had:

- borrowed in international bond markets,
- taken large loans from private credit funds hungry for yield,
- experimented with tokenising some of its debt to reach new investors,
- and surfed the 2020s on a mix of commodity exports, tourism, and short-term foreign capital.

In other words: normal, by modern standards. Until the weekend they shut the pipes.

"Temporary Capital Management Measures"

The first headline hit on a Sunday night, East Coast time:

SAN AURELIO ANNOUNCES TEMPORARY CAPITAL MANAGEMENT MEASURES TO PROTECT FINANCIAL STABILITY

If you've been around long enough, you know this translation: "Capital controls. Something broke." The official statement was textbook:

- "In light of recent pressures on foreign exchange markets…"
- "To safeguard the stability of the financial system…"
- "These temporary measures do not affect the real economy…"

Some of the details sounded eerily familiar to anyone who remembered Cyprus 2013, when bank failures led to strict limits on cash withdrawals, cross-border transfers, and use of bank accounts: no early termination of savings accounts, strict caps on cash taken abroad, spending limits on cards outside the country. San Aurelio's list read like a remix:

- Daily ATM withdrawals capped below what many middle-class households needed for rent and food.
- Wire transfers abroad requiring special approval, with priority given to "essential imports."
- Prohibitions on early redemption of certain high-yield savings products that had been marketed as "flexible."

On paper, it was "temporary." In the real world, it felt like the door slamming shut. Capital controls are not new. Economists have debated them for decades. Post-crisis analyses of episodes in countries like Malaysia after the Asian financial crisis, or Cyprus and

Argentina in their respective turmoil, have argued over whether such controls helped stabilize economies or simply shifted pain around. But whatever the academic verdict, the lived experience is simple: Yesterday, your money could leave. Today, it cannot. Trust does not like that feeling.

How Do You Get to Capital Controls? Slowly, Then All at Once

San Aurelio's crisis didn't begin on that Sunday. It began years earlier, in comfortable conference rooms. For most of the 2020s, global reports kept running the same theme:

- Global public debt levels were "elevated and probably worse than they look," with many countries carrying heavy interest burdens and rising refinancing risks.
- Emerging and developing economies, especially smaller and lower-income ones, remained vulnerable to debt distress as financing costs rose.
- Capital flows to emerging markets slowed compared to the pre-2010 era, with "sudden stops" in some cases—sharp reversals where inflows dried up and outflows surged, often triggering painful adjustments.

You didn't need to be a prophet to see that some of these countries were walking a thin line:

- Borrowing in foreign currency,
- Rolling over short-term debt at higher interest rates,
- Relying on volatile capital flows and commodity prices.

Think about Argentina or Turkey in previous decades: currency slides, sudden stops, external debt pressures, contagion to other emerging markets.

Now layer on several new features unique to the 2020s:

- Private credit loans to governments and quasi-sovereign entities, often with bespoke terms and fewer public disclosures.
- Tokenised government and corporate debt, sold through new platforms to a global pool of investors.
- Global financial conditions that looked calm in the near term, even as IMF and FSB reports warned about medium-term vulnerabilities in sovereign debt and credit markets.

San Aurelio checked all those boxes. As long as global investors were hungry for yield and willing to believe in the story, the country could refinance, extend, pretend, and keep the music going. Until the music changed.

The Straw That Broke the Peg

The immediate trigger, in our story, was almost petty:

- A missed communication on a bond rollover.
- A leaked memo about "fiscal slippage."
- A downgrade rumor circulating on a Friday afternoon.

By Friday evening, San Aurelio's currency was sliding. By Saturday, unconfirmed screenshots of bank queues began circulating online. By Sunday, the central bank announced the "temporary measures."

From the outside, analysts debated whether this was a classic sudden stop—a case where foreign investors lost confidence, capital flows reversed, and the country had to slam the gate to stop the outflow. From the inside, people just saw:

- cards not working,
- online banking glitchy,

- shops putting up "cash only" signs,
- families worrying about remittances and tuition payments.

Internationally, the first reaction was almost bored:

"Moderate sell-off in local markets."

"Regional risk spreads widen modestly."

"Analysts say contagion is limited."

We have heard this lullaby before. In earlier crises—Cyprus in 2013, for instance—commentary out of Europe often suggested that capital controls and bail-ins were unique, contained, and unlikely to spark broader turmoil. Yet studies later documented how the episode rattled investors and contributed to stress in other peripheral eurozone markets, even if the worst-case contagion was avoided.San Aurelio looked, at first, like one more "manageably messy" case.But under the surface, 2029 was not 2013. The wiring was different.

The Web Behind One "Small" Sovereign

By the time San Aurelio pulled the emergency brake, the country's obligations were not just sitting in a neat pile of vanilla bonds on some pension fund's shelf. They were:

- in EM sovereign bond ETFs held by retail investors from Tokyo to Toronto,
- in private credit funds that had lent directly to state-owned firms and infrastructure projects, often at floating rates,
- in tokenised sovereign notes used as collateral on DeFi platforms and in structured products,
- in derivatives and credit default swaps written by global banks and hedge funds.

Global reports leading up to this period had warned that:

- Private credit's growth and rising maturity wall—projected to peak around 2028 with tens of billions in loans coming due—could amplify downturns if refinancing conditions worsened.
- Sovereign debt vulnerabilities, especially in smaller and lower-income countries, were increasing as interest costs rose and hidden debts occasionally came to light.
- Tokenisation and non-bank structures were making linkages between traditional and decentralized finance more complex, with potential for shocks to transmit in new ways.

San Aurelio wasn't the problem. It was simply the point where many problems met.

To borrow a phrase from one IMF report, the world was living in an environment of "apparent calm in a more fragile world"—low realized volatility, but deeper structural vulnerabilities in sovereign debt, credit, and asset valuations. San Aurelio was where the calm slipped.

"That's Weird" – The Market's Favorite Epitaph

On Monday morning, global markets did not immediately panic.

- The local currency tanked.
- San Aurelio's bond prices gapped down.
- Regional ETFs took a hit.

But the big indices? They wobbled, then shrugged. If you were watching carefully, though, you saw a subtler signal:

- Spreads on a cluster of similar countries began to widen.
- Private credit funds with emerging-market exposure

quietly stopped taking new money or delayed redemptions citing "valuation uncertainty."

- A few DeFi protocols suddenly marked certain tokenised sovereign assets as "ineligible collateral."

In the language of financial crises, this is called re-pricing risk. In the language of the church basement, it's called: "The market just realized what time it is."

Academic work on sudden stops and capital flow reversals in emerging markets has shown that these episodes rarely stay neatly contained; investors often reassess risk across a whole category of countries, not just the one in the headlines. Add in 2020s-style complexity—private credit structures, ETFs, derivatives, tokenised assets—and you don't just have a country sneezing. You have the whole category clearing its throat.

What It Looked Like From West Philadelphia

Meanwhile, in our church basement, phones lit up.

One of the WPBS crew sent a screenshot from his trading app, showing a sea of red in an emerging-market bond ETF. "Doc, should we care about this little country? News says it's contained." Another forwarded a DeFi forum thread: "Protocol just disabled a bunch of tokenised sovereigns as collateral. People in the comments are saying 'no big deal' and 'FUD.'"

I pulled up a few things:

- The latest Global Financial Stability Report, which had warned that medium-term vulnerabilities were building in sovereign and corporate debt markets, even as near-term risks looked manageable.
- A recent FSB report on sovereign and NBFI risks, highlighting how smaller emerging economies were

especially exposed to higher financing costs and sudden shifts in investor sentiment.
- Research on private credit's maturity wall, pointing out that a wave of loans was scheduled to roll off around this exact period, forcing funds to either extend, restructure, or liquidate borrowers—just as sovereign stress might hurt those borrowers' revenues.

Then I said the line nobody wants to hear in the middle of a bull market: "It's not about whether San Aurelio is big. It's about what it's plugged into." You don't worry about a single outlet starting to smoke because the outlet is majestic. You worry because it's on the same circuit as your entire first floor.

The Private Credit Dominoes Wiggle

Within days of San Aurelio's controls:

- A regional infrastructure fund with private credit exposure quietly disclosed that "a small number" of its projects had requested covenant waivers.
- A global private credit fund with loans to San Aurelio's state-owned enterprises sent a letter to investors: distribution "pauses," "review of valuation assumptions," "continuing to monitor the situation."
- A rating agency note highlighted that, across emerging markets, about $50 billion in private credit maturities were projected to come due around 2028–2030, exactly when sovereign stress was rising.

None of these events made the front page. But for people who had been reading the footnotes, it felt like watching hairline cracks appear in a plain-looking dam.

Regulators and researchers had been warning for several years that private credit's rapid growth, opacity, and linkages to banks and institutional investors could make it a conduit for systemic risk in a downturn.

The San Aurelio episode didn't prove that thesis. But it provided a live-fire drill.

- If one "small" sovereign's troubles could freeze significant flows,
- what would a cluster of such events do?
- What would it mean if private credit funds couldn't easily roll loans or raise new capital, just as borrowers and governments got squeezed?

Those were not questions the market wanted to answer in public yet. But in back rooms, the spreadsheets started to grow extra tabs.

"Contained" Has a Short Shelf Life

For a while, officials stuck to their usual script: "We are monitoring the situation." "We see no signs of broad contagion." "The global financial system remains resilient." To be fair, they were not lying. Not yet. Markets did not crash that week. The VIX did not spike into the stratosphere. Most people went to work, paid their bills, and scrolled past the San Aurelio story on the way to more entertaining doom. But IMF and FSB commentary around this period had already been emphasizing that even in the absence of immediate crises, sovereign debt, asset valuations, and non-bank vulnerabilities were creating a more fragile backdrop.

In that sense, San Aurelio was less an earthquake and more a foreshock:

- It showed how quickly a mid-tier economy could be pushed into capital controls once confidence slipped.
- It exposed how intertwined such a country's obligations were with private credit, tokenised assets, and global instruments.

- It reminded anyone paying attention that "small" sovereigns can be big enough to destabilize certain corners of the system.
- The phrase "idiosyncratic" got a heavy workout in analyst notes. But history has a sense of humor. "Idiosyncratic" is what we often call the first domino.

The WPBS Takeaway

In the church basement, we updated nothing and everything. We didn't:

- Rush to short emerging-market ETFs.
- Panic about global collapse that week.
- Declare, "This is it, sell everything."

We did:

1. Reaffirm Our Theology of Risk

   Global markets are powerful tools, not stable gods. Their promises are conditional. Their mood can swing from "we'll buy anything" to "we trust no one" faster than any committee can draft a statement.

2. Review Exposure to Fragile Stories

   We checked where our own people had over-reached—chasing yield in products ten layers removed from reality, trusting marketing more than mandates. We didn't ban all EM, all private credit, or all tokenised assets. We simply bumped them farther down the priority list.

3. Strengthen the Real-Economy Core

   We doubled down on the quiet work:

- local businesses that sold actual goods and services,
- co-ops and community-owned housing projects,
- investments in food, energy, health, and data infrastructure that would matter whether or not some distant sovereign restructured its bonds.

4. Pray With Our Eyes Open

   We did what believers ought to do in any storm or pre-storm:

   We prayed.

   Not that markets would forever go up, but that when they went down, we would have wisdom, liquidity, and love enough to respond.

Because here is the uncomfortable truth San Aurelio made visible: In a world that has normalized distrust (Chapter 2), gotten high on tech narratives (Chapter 3), and buried leverage in the shadows (Chapter 4), it doesn't take a giant to shake the room. Sometimes, all it takes is a "small country" sneezing at the wrong moment.

And 2029 was just getting started.

In the next chapter, we move from sovereign headlines to something even more "boring"—a fund so ordinary, so allegedly safe, that people used it like a savings account with better PR. When that instrument flinched, the shadows stopped being theoretical.

2029

Chapter 6

A Very Boring Fund Breaks the World

If you ask regular people what could crash the global financial system, they'll say:

- "A war."
- "A cyberattack."
- "Some billionaire doing something stupid on live TV."

Almost nobody will say: "The CashPlus Enhanced Short Duration Opportunity Fund."And that, right there, is the problem.

Meet the Fund You Never Worried About

The official name was longer, but everybody just called it "CashPlus." It lived in the "low-risk" section of the app. Its logo was soothing blue. Its brochure showed retirees on beaches, couples sipping coffee, and at least one child with a kite. CashPlus was marketed as:

- "Cash-like,"
- "Highly liquid,"
- "Capital preservation with modest yield enhancement."

Translated: "Almost a savings account… just, you know, better." It invested in things the marketing people described as:

- short-term corporate paper,
- high-grade securitizations,
- lightly seasoned private credit,
- select tokenised real-world assets,
- and "opportunistic sovereign exposure."

All wrapped in language about "advanced liquidity management" and "robust risk controls." You know you're in danger when the brochure uses the word "robust."

We've Seen This Movie Before

There is nothing new about a "boring" fund turning into a main character. In 2008, a U.S. money market fund called the Reserve Primary Fund did something that wasn't supposed to happen: after losses on Lehman Brothers' commercial paper, its net asset value fell below $1 per share—"breaking the buck." The drop to 97 cents didn't sound dramatic on its own. But money funds were sold as rock-solid cash equivalents. When one of them failed to maintain $1, investors bolted:

- Prime money market funds saw hundreds of billions in outflows,
- Government money funds saw massive inflows as people rushed for perceived safety,
- The U.S. government ended up backstopping the sector to stop the run.

In March 2020, during the COVID "dash for cash," a different flavor of boring almost broke things again:

- Open-ended bond funds and some money market funds faced heavy outflows,
- Investors raced to redeem at yesterday's price while underlying markets were seizing up,
- Central banks had to step in with huge interventions to stabilize bond markets and funding markets.

Global watchdogs like the Financial Stability Board (FSB), central banks, and the ECB all wrote very serious documents afterward, pointing out that:

- many open-ended funds let investors redeem daily,
- while holding assets that could not be sold quickly without big discounts,
- creating a "liquidity mismatch" and a first-mover advantage for investors who ran early.

The warning was clear: "If you give people the right to leave any time, but you invest their money in things that can't leave, you have built a run machine."

Then, in 2022, the UK gave us the LDI crisis:

- Defined-benefit pension funds using leveraged liability-driven investment (LDI) strategies had to meet huge margin calls when gilt yields spiked after a controversial "mini-budget."
- They scrambled to raise cash, selling long-dated gilts in a fire sale.
- Yields spiraled higher, forcing the Bank of England to step in with an emergency bond-buying program to stop the spiral.

Again: pensions… long-dated government bonds… boring. Until suddenly: systemic.

So by 2029, the idea that a "safe" vehicle could turn dangerous was not hypothetical. The receipts were there. Regulators had revised their recommendations, especially on liquidity mismatch in open-ended funds, and were publicly calling for stronger liquidity management and better tools to reduce run risks. The world read the reports, nodded solemnly, and then poured more money into things that looked exactly like CashPlus.

How CashPlus Was Supposed to Work

On a normal day, CashPlus did something like this:

- Took in a billion dollars from investors who wanted "a little more than cash."
- Bought a stew of assets:
    - very short-term loans to solid companies,
    - slices of securitized loans,
    - some "defensive" private credit exposures,
    - tokenised Treasury-backed notes that could be used in DeFi as collateral,
    - and a sprinkling of "opportunistic" emerging-market paper.
- Promised investors they could get their money out on T+1 (next business day).

Behind the scenes, the fund managers modeled:

- normal flows in and out,
- typical bid-ask spreads in the assets they held,
- stress scenarios based on 2008 and 2020,
- lines of credit they could tap if things got choppy.

On paper, it was conservative. In marketing, it was comforting. In reality, it was leveraged trust. Because every daily NAV, every redemption promise, depended on a simple assumption: "In stressed markets, we will still be able to sell enough stuff, at sane prices, fast enough." You already know where this is going.

After San Aurelio, the Water Got Cloudy

When San Aurelio slammed on capital controls (Chapter 5), the shock was "moderate but manageable" in the headlines. Inside CashPlus, it was… awkward. They weren't massively exposed to San Aurelio's government bonds. They were exposed to things connected to San Aurelio:

- A regional infrastructure project securitization,
- A private loan to a quasi-sovereign utility,
- A tokenised note backed by a basket of frontier sovereigns.

Nothing huge in isolation. But valuations got fuzzy:

- Secondary markets went illiquid.
- Dealers widened spreads or said, "call me Thursday."
- Pricing services started flagging more positions as "level 3"—valued by models, not market quotes.

Meanwhile, jittery investors who saw the San Aurelio headlines began reallocating:

- Some sold their emerging-market bond funds outright.
- Some trimmed anything that mentioned "frontier," "opportunistic," or "plus."
- Some just decided, "You know what, I'd rather sit in plain T-bills for a while."

CashPlus saw outflows. Not catastrophic. Just steady and one-directional. To meet redemptions, they sold the easiest, most liquid holdings:

- Treasuries,
- top-tier commercial paper,
- tokenised T-bill instruments that traded actively on-chain.

This left a higher concentration of hard-to-sell stuff in the fund—exactly the opposite of what you want when people are nervous. It's the grocery store problem: If everyone buys the good bread first, the shelf ends up full of stale rolls nobody wants.

The Day the Gate Came Down

The formal tipping point came on a Wednesday morning. Overnight, a rumor had swept through a few finance subreddits and encrypted group chats: someone claimed CashPlus had tapped its bank credit line. That alone was not unusual; funds use credit lines all the time to smooth flows. But in a fragile trust environment (Chapter 2), context doesn't matter.

Phones lit up. Advisors got emails: "Should I be worried?" Corporate treasurers, who had parked surplus cash in CashPlus for extra yield, quietly submitted big redemption orders—"just to be safe." By late morning, the fund's risk committee had three ugly facts:

1. Outflows were running at several times normal levels.
2. The liquid buffer was nearly exhausted.
3. Selling more illiquid assets into a thin market would mean fire-sale prices that hammered the remaining investors.

They also had a lawyer in the corner pointing at a page no one had paid attention to when times were good: "In exceptional circumstances, the Fund may impose redemption gates, suspend redemptions, or use other liquidity management tools to protect remaining shareholders." And so, with a press release that would later be dissected in business schools and congressional hearings, CashPlus announced:

- "Temporary suspension of redemptions,"
- "In order to ensure fair and orderly treatment of all investors,"
- "While we conduct a prudent review of portfolio valuation in light of recent market conditions."

Translated: "You can't have your money right now. Please remain calm."

How a Boring Fund Becomes a Signal

Technically, this was not the first time a fund had gated investors.

We've had episodes for decades where open-ended property funds froze withdrawals, credit funds gated redemptions, and hedge funds locked up capital. In some crises, UK commercial property funds, for example, suspended trading after big shocks like Brexit or market downturns, citing fairness and liquidity issues.

Regulators and the FSB had specifically warned that funds with liquidity mismatch might need stronger tools—like swing pricing, redemption gates, and notice periods—to avoid panicked fire sales that spill into the broader system. But CashPlus was different in one crucial way: It sat in the "cash and short-term" bucket in millions of mental balance sheets. People didn't think of it as a risky hedge fund or a niche product. They thought of it as:

- where payroll money rested between runs,
- where churches parked building funds,
- where municipalities kept operating surpluses,
- where families stored emergency savings that "deserved a little more than zero."

When that type of fund says, "See you later," the message isn't just: "This one product has an issue." The message is: "You can't fully trust the line between 'cash' and 'just-like-cash' anymore." And in a trust-fragile world, that line was the last comfort blanket many people had.

Echoes of 2008 and 2020

The parallels were uncomfortable. In 2008, Reserve Primary broke the buck, triggering a wider run on money funds and forcing the U.S. government to guarantee the sector temporarily.

In March 2020, the "dash for cash" showed again how quickly investors would flee from anything that wasn't pure government-backed, causing strains in even the safest bond markets and pushing open-ended funds with liquidity mismatch into stress.

Post-mortems from central banks, the FDIC, the FSB, and others highlighted the same vulnerabilities over and over:

- Liquidity mismatch between daily redemption promises and slower-moving assets,
- First-mover advantage—redeem early and you get out at a better price, leaving losses for those who wait,
- Interconnectedness with core funding and sovereign bond markets,
- Reliance on central banks as emergency backstops for non-bank markets.

By late 2023, the FSB and IOSCO had rolled out revised policy recommendations to strengthen liquidity management in open-ended funds, aiming to reduce the likelihood of runs. In the lab, the diagnosis was clear. In the wild, CashPlus still happened. Because policy moves slow. Incentives move fast. And yield temptation moves faster.

Contagion in Three Steps

Once CashPlus gated, the sequence was brutally simple:

1. Re-labeling Risk

   Investors everywhere looked at anything labeled "cash-plus," "enhanced," or "short-duration opportunity" and thought:

   "If that one can freeze, maybe mine can too."

   Outflows hit similar funds. Some pre-emptively raised gates or fees. Others were forced into fire sales.

2. Collateral Chains Snap

   Some stablecoins and DeFi protocols had parked reserves or collateral in CashPlus-like vehicles—especially tokenised short-term credit portfolios marketed as safe yield sources.

When redemptions froze and valuations got murky, those protocols had to:

- ◦ mark collateral down,
- ◦ restrict withdrawals,
- ◦ or trigger margin calls on users.

TradFi's little gate became DeFi's big problem.

3. Dash for Real Cash

   Corporate treasurers, foundations, municipalities, and plain households did the obvious thing:

   - ◦ Move money back into plain bank deposits.
   - ◦ Shift into direct T-bill purchases or government money funds only.
   - ◦ Cancel or delay planned investments and spending "until it all blows over."

In other words: a 2029 version of the dash for cash, but this time starting from the shadows instead of a virus. Bond markets felt it. Repo markets felt it. Cross-border funding channels felt it. And the machines absolutely felt it.

The Algorithms Smell Smoke

AI-driven trading systems didn't care about CashPlus's beach-photo brochure. They saw:

- rising correlations among short-duration credit spreads,
- stress in tokenised short-term instruments,
- widening bid-ask spreads in multiple "cash-plus" products,
- and a sharp increase in search, social, and news mentions of "gating," "suspensions," and "liquidity tools."

To them, this looked eerily like a run-in-slow-motion on a whole category of funds that many models had treated as nearly cash-equivalent. So they adjusted:

- marking up probability of funding stress,
- marking down assumptions about liquidity,
- and quietly reducing exposures to anything that smelled like "runnable promise backed by not-so-runnable assets."

It's not that the algorithms "panicked." They simply updated the math. But when enough large, fast players update the math at once, the effect—on spreads, on volumes, on prices—is indistinguishable from a coordinated flinch.

How It Looked in the Church Basement

On the day CashPlus gated, one of our WPBS folks walked into the basement with that look. Not the "help me, I lost everything" look. The "I just realized my 'conservative' option wasn't actually conservative" look. He said: "Doc, this was the fund my corporate job recommended for our short-term cash.

We thought we were being prudent. We picked the boring option." I nodded."Boring," I said, "is only safe if it's boring all the way down." We pulled up:

- FDIC speeches talking about non-bank open-end funds and liquidity mismatch as structural vulnerabilities that can create run incentives.
- FSB and central bank reports noting that in March 2020, some funds used liquidity management tools successfully, while others saw tools like swing pricing and gating accelerate redemptions by signaling deeper trouble.
- Fresh headlines about our current "temporary suspension" and "continued monitoring" from authorities who

sounded calm but who, if you read between the lines, were awake at 3 a.m.

Then we did what WPBS had been built to do:

1. Separate Signal from Sensation

   We didn't assume every product would fail. But we did accept a hard truth:

   The boundary between "cash" and "not-quite-cash" is much more fragile than people want to admit.

2. Check Our Own House

   We verified where our churches, families, and small businesses had parked money. If they'd been lured into "safe-ish" funds they didn't understand, we planned exits—careful, not panicked.

3. Reaffirm the Core

   We reminded ourselves why we had built portfolios anchored in:

   - direct government bills and deposits,
   - real assets in our communities,
   - equity in businesses that produced essentials,
   - and adequate plain cash for emergencies.

4. Prepare for the Second-Order Hits

   We knew CashPlus itself was not the whole crisis. But we could already see what was coming:

   - tighter credit to small businesses,
   - more volatile funding for local governments,
   - stressed DeFi protocols spilling hurt onto retail users,

    - nervous corporates cutting spending and hiring "until conditions normalize."

So we prayed, we planned, and yes, we laughed—because if you don't find some humor in a world where a fund with a kite on the brochure can shake the system, you will lose your mind.

When Plumbing Becomes the Main Plot

In every big crisis, there's a moment when the plot shifts from the glamorous to the plumbing.

- In 2008, it was money funds and repo.
- In 2020, it was bond fund liquidity and dollar funding.
- In 2022 UK, it was LDI collateral calls and long-dated gilts.
- In 2029, in this story, it is CashPlus and its cousins.

A boring fund halting redemptions does not sound like the apocalypse. Until you realize:

- that fund sat at the crossroads of households, corporates, DeFi, and sovereign debt;
- that its structure was modeled on patterns regulators had been worrying about for years;
- and that its failure to live up to the "almost cash" story shattered the last, fragile illusion of safety for millions of people already living in a distrustful, over-leveraged, AI-amplified world.

The official histories will later call it "a liquidity event in a segment of non-bank financial intermediation." The people who lived it will call it: "The week we realized even our boring was broken."

And remember: for WPBS, this is not the end of the world. It is the confirmation that the world we quietly planned for—the volatile, low-trust, regime-shifting one—is now fully here.

In the next chapter, we turn to the other shoe dropping:

The stablecoin that was supposed to be the safe digital harbor—regulator-friendly, fully backed, audited, "for adults"— and what happened when its peg slipped on the very week everyone needed something, anything, to stay exactly at $1.00.

2029

Chapter 7

The Stablecoin That Wasn't

The world really wanted just one thing to stay at $1.00. Stocks could swing. Bonds could wobble. AI coins could moon and crash on the same Tuesday. But surely—surely—there had to be some digital token, some clean piece of code, that would hold a steady line at one U.S. dollar, no matter what. By 2029, that comforting fantasy had a name: GDS – the Global Digital Settlement Dollar. The marketing tagline was better: "The world's most trusted digital dollar." Bless their hearts.

A Short History of "Don't Worry, It's Stable"

To understand how much faith people put in GDS, it helps to remember what came before it. The first big wave of stablecoins was basically: "Look, we promise it's backed. Trust us. Also here's a cute whitepaper." They came in a few flavors:

1. Fiat-backed in a bank –

   "We hold real dollars in a real bank. You get one coin per dollar."

2. Crypto-backed on-chain –

   "We lock volatile crypto in a smart contract. You mint a stablecoin. The extra collateral absorbs the swings."

3. Algorithmic –

   "We have math and vibes. No, seriously, it's complicated, but it'll be fine."

You know the rest.

In May 2022, the TerraUSD / LUNA experiment—an algorithmic stablecoin pegged to $1 via a burn-and-mint relationship with its sister token—collapsed in a matter of days. LUNA went from over $100 to essentially zero, wiping out roughly $45–50 billion in combined market value and contributing to hundreds of billions in wider crypto losses. Terra's design did not rely on traditional collateral backing; it relied on:

- market incentives,
- an associated yield platform (Anchor),
- and faith that the algorithmic mechanism would always work.

When that faith broke, the peg went with it. Later investigations and court proceedings painted an ugly picture: misleading claims about stability and safety, massive investor losses, and eventually fraud charges against Terra's founder. The message was clear: Algorithmic "trust me bro" is not a balance sheet. But the industry didn't quit. It pivoted.

Then the "Good" Stablecoins Flinched Too

If Terra was the wild child, USDC was marketed as the diligent honor student. Fully reserved. Regulated partners. Audited statements. Used by institutions as on- and off-ramps.

Then Silicon Valley Bank failed in March 2023—the largest U.S. bank failure since 2008. SVB had loaded up on long-duration securities; when rates rose and depositors ran, the hole became visible and the bank went into receivership. Circle, USDC's issuer, disclosed that $3.3 billion of its roughly $40 billion reserves were stuck at SVB when the bank went down. Markets didn't wait for a resolution:

- USDC, designed to stay at $1, dropped to around $0.88 at its low on some exchanges.
- Arbitrageurs, panicked holders, and bots all scrambled at once.
- Only after regulators backstopped SVB's depositors did USDC fully regain its peg.

So even a "fully backed, regulated, dollars-in-a-bank" stablecoin was only as stable as:

- the banks,
- the disclosure,
- and the speed of the political response.

Then there was Tether (USDT)—the OG "don't worry about it" coin. For years, critics raised questions about its reserves: How much was in cash? How much in commercial paper? How much in riskier loans?

In 2021, the U.S. Commodity Futures Trading Commission fined Tether $41 million, finding that it had made misleading statements about being fully backed by U.S. dollars at all times between 2016 and 2018. Under pressure, Tether shifted its reserve composition:

- By 2022–24, it claimed to have eliminated commercial paper entirely, moving heavily into U.S. Treasury bills and other liquid assets, with public reserve attestations.

Yet concerns about transparency, governance, and risk management never fully disappeared. Rating agencies and commentators highlighted opacity in disclosures and potential vulnerabilities if risky assets in reserves dropped in value.

The lesson? Even "successful" stablecoins are not magically stable. They are small, leveraged replicas of the financial system they sit on.

The Adults Enter the Room (Sort Of)

After Terra, FTX, and a cascade of lesser freak-outs, the adults in dark suits convened.

The Financial Stability Board (FSB) laid out high-level recommendations for global stablecoin regulation in 2020–23, emphasizing:

- robust reserve backing,
- clear redemption rights,
- strong governance,
- and consistent oversight across borders.

In 2023 the FSB finalized a global regulatory framework for crypto-asset activities, including stablecoins, endorsed by the G20. A 2025 thematic review stressed that rapid crypto growth made full implementation urgent, especially for tokens that could be used at scale across countries.

The IMF, meanwhile, published detailed work on stablecoins, describing:

- their potential benefits for payments and inclusion,
- their differences from traditional money and bank deposits,
- and the regulatory requirements needed to mitigate risks to monetary policy, capital flows, and financial stability.

Everybody agreed—on paper—that if a stablecoin was going to be used widely, it needed:

- high-quality, liquid backing assets,
- segregation and protection of reserves,
- transparent, frequent reporting,
- strong risk management and operational resilience,
- and clear legal frameworks.

Out of that new, heavily negotiated regulatory soup emerged a handful of "Tier 1" compliant stablecoins. GDS was the star.

GDS: The Good Child of Stablecoins

GDS wasn't just a crypto project; it was a policy darling.

- Structured in multiple jurisdictions with licensed entities.
- Backed—on paper—by a mix of short-term government bonds, bank deposits, and tokenised high-grade instruments.
- Integrated into major payment networks, exchanges, and DeFi platforms.
- Used by corporates for cross-border settlements, especially in regions frustrated with the cost and friction of the legacy correspondent banking system.

If early stablecoins were "move fast and break things," GDS was "move carefully and brief the regulators first." Whitepapers and policy blogs used phrases like:

- "Programmable wholesale settlement."
- "Compliant cross-border rails."
- "Tokenised reserve transparency."

Consultants wrote reports about how GDS and similar regulated stablecoins could:

- lower remittance costs,
- speed up trade payments,
- and reduce reliance on weaker local banking systems.

Real-world developments pointed in that direction:

- Experimentation with stablecoins for cross-border trade in sanctioned or dollar-constrained regions.
- Growing use of tokenised T-bill products as on-chain cash equivalents.

GDS rode that wave. It was the stablecoin you could mention in polite company. Where early adopters once bragged about Bitcoin, 2028 corporate treasurers casually referenced their "GDS float". And then 2029 happened.

The Hidden Plumbing of GDS

On the surface, the GDS reserve breakdown looked clean:

- 60%: short-term U.S. and core sovereign bills, held in segregated accounts.
- 20%: bank deposits at "highly rated" institutions across several countries.
- 15%: tokenised T-bill and repo instruments, some used for intraday liquidity.
- 5%: "cash-plus" liquidity products and highly rated short-duration credit.

If someone squinted, they might notice that last bucket. After the CashPlus gate (Chapter 6), GDS published a short statement: "We have no material exposure to the specific fund currently in the news. Our use of short-duration credit products remains well within conservative limits." The word "material" did a lot of work in that sentence. What the statement did not emphasize:

- Some of the "cash-plus" exposures sat in vehicles that held similar underlying assets to CashPlus—short-term private credit, securitised loans, and tokenised sovereign notes.
- A non-trivial portion of GDS's bank deposits were with institutions that themselves had significant ties to non-bank funding markets and tokenised asset platforms.
- A slice of the reserve's tokenised T-bill and repo instruments were rehypothecated—used as collateral in

other transactions in ways that made access slower in stress.

In fairness, none of that was obviously reckless. It was standard 2020s-level "sophisticated liquidity management." GDS's own documentation listed the risks:

- market risk on reserves,
- credit risk on banking partners,
- operational risk in custodians and smart contracts,
- legal risk across jurisdictions.

But in a world desperate for something to treat as digital cash, most users just heard, "Fully backed. Supervised. Boring." They treated GDS as water, not realizing it flowed through pipes that had already started to rattle.

The Rumor That Popped the $1 Illusion

The trigger was simple and, like many triggers, partially wrong. An anonymized research note—part leaked internal memo, part external analysis—started circulating among funds and large traders. It claimed that:

- GDS held "up to 8–10%" of its reserves in funds similar to CashPlus,
- GDS had significant exposure to two regional banks under market stress,
- and some of its tokenised reserves were locked in facilities facing margin calls.

The actual numbers were messier and less dramatic. But by then, the CashPlus gate had already scared people. The San Aurelio episode (Chapter 5) had reawakened sovereign risk fears. And years of stablecoin drama—from Terra's implosion to USDC's SVB depeg to ongoing questions about Tether—had trained traders to respond quickly. So when the rumor landed, the market did what the market does best: It ran before it read.

On a Tuesday afternoon:

- GDS started trading at $0.997 on one large exchange.
- Then $0.993.
- Then, on a venue with thinner liquidity and more leveraged users, $0.97.

Arbitrage desks moved in, buying the discount and redeeming with GDS's issuer for $1 in reserves. But that game only works smoothly if:

- redemption windows are fully open,
- settlement is fast,
- and nobody is panicking about the reserves themselves.

This time, those conditions failed.

Redemption, Meet Reality

As redemptions surged:

- Some of GDS's bank partners hit internal exposure limits and slowed wire-outs.
- A portion of tokenised T-bill positions, held via on-chain structures with off-chain custodians, faced delays as collateral arrangements were reassessed.
- Several "cash-plus" products in the reserve pool applied their own liquidity tools—swing pricing, larger spreads, or partial gates.

On-chain, people saw:

- GDS slipping to $0.95 in some DeFi pools.
- Protocols raising collateral requirements for GDS-backed borrowing.

- Risk dashboards lighting up with "peg deviation" alerts.

Off-chain, they saw:

- social feeds filling with screenshots of the price,
- pundits who had spent two years saying "GDS is the grown-up stablecoin" suddenly going quiet,
- and a flood of corporate treasurers calling their banks.

In one sense, the situation was still far from Terra:

- GDS had real assets backing it—sovereign bills, deposits, short-term paper.
- GDS was not collapsing toward zero; it was wobbling in the low-90-cent range.
- If given enough time, it could probably have liquidated assets and honored redemptions at or near par.

But markets do not grant "enough time" when the collective mood is: "I don't want to be the last fool holding the bag."

Academic analyses of the USDC-SVB episode later noted how quickly stablecoin prices moved away from $1 once confidence wavered, even though underlying reserves were largely intact and eventually accessible.Now multiply that behavior by:

- a larger stablecoin,
- more integration with DeFi and TradFi,
- and a world already on edge from CashPlus and San Aurelio.

Code vs. Law, Round Two

As the GDS peg slipped, a fascinating clash re-emerged: Code says one thing. Law says another. On-chain:

- Smart contracts treated 1 GDS as whatever the market said it was at that moment.

- Loans collateralized by GDS auto-liquidated when borrowers fell below thresholds.
- Automated trading bots arbitraged every price difference they could see.

Off-chain:

- Legislators and regulators called emergency meetings.
- There was talk—again—of "temporary measures" to support stablecoin confidence, possibly including:
    - central bank swap lines,
    - emergency liquidity backstops for qualifying issuers,
    - fast-track interventions in key banks and funds holding reserves.

FSB and IMF documents had already warned that stablecoins used at scale could create pressures on capital flows, monetary policy, and financial stability—especially if they faced runs or were used extensively for cross-border transactions.

A 2024 joint IMF–FSB roadmap for crypto-asset policy implementation emphasized the need to coordinate oversight of global stablecoin arrangements, particularly in emerging markets, to avoid destabilizing spillovers. Now, in 2029, that scenario wasn't in a PDF. It was on the screen. Governments were forced to decide:

- Would they backstop a privately issued digital token because it had become too important to fail?
- Would they let the market sort it out and risk contagion to payments, DeFi, and funding markets?
- Would they ringfence, nationalize, or outright replace GDS with central bank digital currencies (CBDCs) in some corridors?

Some argued: "If we bail out this thing, we socialize losses for a private experiment. Others countered: "If we let it fail chaotically, we risk a payments seizure and a deeper crisis." Meanwhile, the smart contracts didn't care. They just kept liquidating.

Flight to... What, Exactly?

For ordinary users, the experience was brutally simple:

- Yesterday, 1 GDS was a digital dollar.
- Today, 1 GDS is... 0.91? 0.94? Depends where you look.

They didn't have the bandwidth to parse FSB recommendations or balance sheet footnotes. They just knew that the thing everyone told them was "as good as cash" was suddenly trading like a penny stock on a bad day. So the flight began—again:

- Into plain bank deposits, despite recent memories of banks failing.
- Into direct government T-bills, often via tokenised platforms that at least gave the feeling of direct exposure.
- Into Bitcoin and a handful of other hard-capped assets, not because they were stable, but because some people decided they'd rather take volatility risk than governance risk.
- Into physical cash, especially in countries where banking systems had recently shown their own instability.

International research on previous runs, like USDC's SVB depeg, had already suggested that stablecoin stumbles could prompt shifts between different forms of money, affecting both crypto and traditional funding markets. Now those findings were playing out in the wild at a larger scale.

How It Looked from the Church Basement

In West Philly, nobody was shocked that a stablecoin could slip. Terra had already taught the world that "algorithmic" wasn't a synonym for "immortal." USDC's SVB episode had shown that even well-structured coins depended on bank risk and policy response speed. Tether's long-running drama reminded everyone that opacity plus scale is its own risk factor. What the GDS wobble drove home was simpler: "There is no digital escape hatch from real-world fragility. The rails may be new. The risks are very old."

In one WPBS session, we wrote on the whiteboard:

- Cash in hand – risk: inflation, theft, opportunity cost.
- Bank deposits – risk: bank failure, bail-ins, capital controls, deposit limits.
- Government bills – risk: sovereign default, inflation, market volatility.
- Stablecoins – risk: all of the above, plus smart-contract, operational, and regulatory risk.

Then we added our conclusion: "None of these is God. All of these are tools."

WPBS didn't swear off stablecoins. Rails are rails. Fast, programmable settlement has real value. But we drew hard lines:

- No treating any stablecoin as the ultimate store of value.
- No assuming 1:1 is a law of nature.
- No building community survival on instruments that depend on ten layers of faith, politics, and plumbing.

We treated GDS, and its cousins, like we would treat a good car:

- Use it.
- Maintain it.
- Insure it.
- Never confuse it with your actual life.

Why GDS Was the Turning Point

CashPlus rattled markets because it showed that "cash-ish" funds could gate. GDS shook something deeper:

- It blurred the line between "money" and "investment product" in the public mind.
- It exposed the fragility of wholesale and retail payments that had quietly shifted onto private rails.

It forced regulators to confront the question: "If this token is important enough that its failure could destabilize the system, why did we let a private consortium run it?"

The FSB's earlier work had warned that global stablecoins could fragment monetary sovereignty, complicate capital flows, and create run risks that spill over into banking systems. In 2029, that paragraph walked off the page and into the street. For everyone else in this book, GDS's stumble is one more tremor in a year of increasingly frequent shocks. For WPBS, it is another confirmation: "Design for a world where trust in systems is conditional. Build for the day when even the 'safest' digital promises wobble. Own what you can see, touch, and govern locally. Use the rest with humility." Because while the world was arguing about whose dollar was real— on-chain, off-chain, programmable, central-bank-issued, privately issued— the algorithms were staring at liquidity data,

the bond markets were staring at spreads, and the clock on the 2029 cascade was ticking louder.

In the next chapter, we step fully into Crash Week:

The machines stop nibbling and start selling, risk models built on calmer decades implode, and human decision-makers discover that by the time they draft a statement, their systems have already moved on.

2029

Chapter 8

Crash Week: When the Machines Flinched First

If you were just glancing at the headlines that Monday morning, Crash Week looked… normal-for-2029:

- "Markets Mixed After Volatile Week"
- "Officials Reassure: Contagion From CashPlus 'Manageable'"
- "GDS Team Reaffirms Commitment to $1 Peg"

In the church basement, our phones were already preaching a different gospel. Indicators that usually move like church mothers—slow, dignified—started twitching like toddlers after red Kool-Aid. Correlations that normally wander in and out of the room lined up in formation. Volumes surged in places that should've been quiet. It didn't look like panic yet. It looked like the machines had quietly decided to be somewhere else.

We Were Warned by the Rehearsal Crashes

Crash Week 2029 didn't come out of a clear blue sky. It came after a decade of dress rehearsals that we applauded, analyzed, and then promptly forgot.

Back in 2010, the U.S. experienced the original "Flash Crash." In the space of about 15 minutes on May 6, major equity indexes dropped roughly 7–9%, temporarily erasing around a trillion dollars of market value before sharply rebounding. Some stocks traded for a penny; others printed absurd prices over $100,000. A joint report from the SEC and CFTC later described how a large, rapid futures sell order collided with fragile liquidity and algorithmic trading, producing a feedback loop: liquidity disappeared, prices plunged, and then bounced back once order books refilled.

In the years that followed, central bankers and market observers noted a series of "flash events":

- the 2010 equity flash crash
- a 2014 "flash rally" in U.S. Treasuries
- other sudden, unexplained moves in major markets

Speeches out of places like the Bank of England and BIS pointed to high-frequency and algorithmic trading interacting with modern market structure to produce sudden spikes and drops that traditional models struggled to explain.

Then came March 2020.

Fear over COVID-19 and policy responses pushed the S&P 500 down so fast that the market-wide circuit breakers—introduced after the 1987 crash—tripped four times in one month. On March 9, 12, 16, and 18, U.S. stocks hit the 7% decline threshold, halting trading for 15 minutes each time to slow the rout. The lesson from all those episodes was clear in the post-mortems:

- Automated strategies can accelerate moves when they all respond to the same signals.
- Liquidity that looks deep in calm periods can evaporate in seconds under stress.
- Circuit breakers can pause the drama, but they can't change the script if the fundamentals are shaky.

Researchers and regulators spent the 2010s and 2020s writing careful papers about how algorithmic trading, high-frequency strategies, and modern order books can both improve liquidity in normal times and amplify volatility in extreme conditions. Those papers lived in PDF folders labeled "risk." In 2029, they jumped onto everybody's home screen.

By 2029, AI Was the Market

By the late 2020s, "algorithmic trading" didn't just mean a few formulas running in the background.

We had:

- Machine-learning models scanning news, earnings calls, social media, and even satellite data for tradeable patterns.
- Reinforcement-learning agents constantly adjusting strategies based on live feedback.
- End-to-end AI pipelines that could ingest data, generate forecasts, construct portfolios, and execute trades—all with minimal human intervention.

Academic work leading up to that period documented how AI and machine learning had become deeply embedded in trading and investment strategies, improving speed and predictive power but also creating new complexity and risk.

Researchers warned that:

- AI systems can learn similar patterns, leading to herding when models trained on overlapping data and objectives all respond in similar ways.
- Complex AI-driven strategies may introduce new tail risks, with interactions that are hard for humans—and even supervisors—to anticipate.

By 2029, estimates suggested that the vast majority of trading volume in major markets was initiated or steered by algorithmic and AI-enhanced systems—an evolution of trends already visible in the

2010s and 2020s. Humans still wrote the objectives:

- "Keep my volatility below X."
- "Stay within this risk budget."
- "Target this tracking error."
- "Dump anything that looks like that crisis over there."

But once those objectives were coded, the machines handled the details—deciding what to sell, when, and how much faster than any human could respond. So when CashPlus gated (Chapter 6) and GDS wobbled (Chapter 7), a huge portion of the global market didn't react with feelings. It reacted with math.

The Pattern the Models Couldn't Ignore

From the AI's point of view, the world suddenly lit up with familiar danger signals:

- Liquidity stress in "cash-plus" funds that were supposed to be nearly cash-equivalent.
- A regulated stablecoin trading below par across multiple venues.
- Widening spreads in short-duration credit and tokenised T-bill instruments, the very things risk models treated as safe collateral.
- Growing volatility in emerging-market sovereigns after San Aurelio's capital controls.

Some of these patterns resembled past episodes:

- the early moments of the 2010 flash crash and other "flash events," where liquidity thinned and prices jumped in odd ways,
- the "dash for cash" in March 2020, when investors sold even safe assets to raise dollars.

But now, the training data included all those prior crises. AI systems had been fed:

- order book data from 2010,
- volatility spikes from 2014,
- circuit-breaker days from 2020,
- and more recent mini-panics in 2024–25.

Academic and policy literature had already speculated that widespread use of AI in trading could alter systemic risk—creating scenarios where models, learning from the same history, might react in correlated ways to stress, amplifying moves rather than damping them.

So, as Crash Week began, many AI-driven strategies quietly shifted into de-risk mode:

- Cutting exposure to anything that looked like "liquidity transformation with daily promises" (funds like CashPlus and its cousins).
- Reducing positions in instruments highly dependent on stablecoin smoothness (GDS-linked credit and tokenised repos).
- Raising cash in the most liquid markets they could find—selling index futures, large-cap equities, and vanilla credit ETFs.

In other words: Before humans panicked, the machines prudently sold the easiest stuff. Which is exactly what you'd program them to do… right up until everybody's "prudence" becomes the problem.

Monday: The Market Feels "Off"

The first day of Crash Week didn't look like a horror movie. It looked like a glitchy Zoom call.

- Bid–ask spreads widened just a bit on major ETFs.
- Index futures gapped more than usual between sessions.
- Correlations across asset classes started rising toward 1 in the stress dashboards.

Commentators blamed it on:

- "Positioning after a volatile week."
- "Technical factors following the GDS news."
- "Traders still digesting the CashPlus situation."

On the exchange floors, though, veteran traders felt that old familiar chill: "This doesn't trade like humans are in charge." Market structure veterans remembered the flash crash literature: how under stress, high-speed strategies can withdraw from providing liquidity, causing prices to gap, followed by rapid rebounds or further cascades. But unlike 2010, the underlying news wasn't just a single large futures order gone wrong. It was:

- cracks in "cash-equivalent" funds,
- doubts about a flagship stablecoin,
- and sovereign stress in the background.

So when prices dipped, there wasn't the same confidence that a swift rebound was guaranteed. This time, the drop felt less like a glitch and more like a preview.

Tuesday: The Circuit Breakers Get Involved

By Tuesday, the selling was no longer subtle. AI risk engines had completed their overnight recalibrations:

- higher volatility inputs,
- higher correlations,
- lower assumptions about liquidity and funding reliability.

That meant lower position limits for any strategy bound by Value-at-Risk or similar metrics. In plain language: "Your models now think this is more dangerous. So they automatically tell you to own less of almost everything." The fastest way to shrink exposure is to sell index futures and big, liquid names. So that's what many AI-steered funds did—almost simultaneously.

By mid-morning, the major U.S. index had fallen far enough, fast enough, to flirt with Level 1 circuit breaker territory—around a 7% intraday decline from the prior close, the threshold set after 1987 and used in March 2020. News tickers started running one of the scariest phrases in finance: "Markets approach circuit-breaker levels."

When the line finally crossed, trading halted for 15 minutes across major U.S. exchanges— just as it had multiple times during the COVID crash years earlier. Circuit breakers, as educational pieces and brokerage explainers like to remind us, exist to pause panic selling, allow information to flow, and give participants time to regroup. But there was a crucial difference in 2029:

- In 1987, 2010, and even 2020, most of the action was on a handful of centralized venues.
- By 2029, trading had spread across:
    - multiple equity and derivatives exchanges,
    - dark pools and internalizers,
    - and a vast 24/7 universe of tokenised assets and derivatives.

You can halt the main theater.bYou cannot halt the entire internet. While the official market paused, activity shifted:

- to offshore venues still open,
- to synthetic positions in tokenised index trackers,
- to stablecoin and crypto pairs that represented proxy bets on what stocks would do when they reopened.

So even during the "calm," the pressure kept building.

The Human Delay

Inside central banks and regulators, phones rang and inboxes exploded. Committees convened. Drafts of statements circulated. Somebody somewhere prepared the classic lines:

- "The financial system remains resilient."
- "We see no disorderly market functioning at this time."
- "We stand ready to use our tools as appropriate."

In fairness, they had learned from past crises:

- Post-1987, they created circuit breakers for major equity indices.
- Post-2010, they studied the flash crash and made adjustments to order handling and trading halts.
- Post-2020, they reviewed the role of algorithmic trading and high-speed strategies during volatility spikes, and refined the rules again.

But all those fixes assumed a world where humans set the pace.

In Crash Week, the problem wasn't that policymakers were lazy or blind. The problem was that, by the time a committee finished debating a sentence, AI-driven flows had already:

- rebalanced portfolios,
- dumped billions in risk assets,
- tripped multiple volatility thresholds,
- and forced leveraged players into margin calls.

They were playing chess in analog. The machines were playing speed chess in 4K.

How It Felt in West Philly

Here's the thing: crashes don't arrive all at once in people's lives. They arrive in notifications:

- A text from HR: "We're reviewing budgets; more info soon."
- An email from a broker: "Due to market conditions, your margin requirements have changed."
- A message from the bank: "We're experiencing higher than usual call volumes."
- A friend at another church: "Our building fund just lost 8% in two days. What do we do?"

We watched from the basement as tickers flashed numbers most people would never see directly, and then watched the translation into ordinary life:

- The small business owner whose line of credit was suddenly frozen.
- The retiree whose "conservative" portfolio dropped enough to keep her awake at night.
- The young programmer whose stock options—her imagined ticket out of debt—deflated just as layoffs started.

We reminded our people: "The market is not your master. It is not your identity. It is not your future. It is not your God." But we didn't say it with fake calm.

We said it with the urgency of someone who sees a hurricane moving fast and knows that even prepared houses will rattle. WPBS wasn't designed to stop volatility. It was designed to survive volatility and to serve in volatility:

- to have some cash when others are forced to sell,
- to own local assets that don't trade tick-by-tick on an exchange,
- to maintain community supports when government budgets start to wobble.

Crash Week was the moment we found out if all those quiet years of planning would matter.

Why This Crash Wasn't Just Another Flash

In earlier episodes like the 2010 flash crash, prices plunged and then bounced back within minutes. The post-crisis ETFs and quant funds soaked up the lesson: "If you can stomach the dip, there's money in the snapback." But by 2029, the context was different:

- Trust in institutions and data had eroded over years (Chapter 2).
- A real-but-over-narrated AI boom had pumped valuations and infrastructure spending to ambitious levels (Chapter 3).
- Shadow banking and non-banks held nearly half the world's financial assets, with known liquidity mismatches and leverage (Chapter 4).
- A "small country" suddenly hitting capital controls showed how fragile some sovereigns really were (Chapter 5).
- "Cash-plus" funds and a flagship stablecoin had just reminded everyone that the line between "safe" and "not-safe" was blurry (Chapters 6 & 7).

So when prices fell in Crash Week, the question wasn't: "Is this a glitch we can fade?" It was: "Is this the moment the stories finally have to match the balance sheets?" That's why, as the week went on, you didn't see the clean, V-shaped rebound of the 2010 flash crash.

You saw:

- halting, algorithm-driven rallies that sold off again,
- multiple circuit breaker trips in different markets,
- and risk-off flows that felt more like 2008 and March 2020 than like a "technical event."

This wasn't just a hiccup in the plumbing. This was the pressure in the pipes finally showing up in the water bill.

The WPBS Lens on the Machines

In one of our evening sessions during Crash Week, somebody asked: "Doc, is AI the villain here?" I smiled, tired. "AI," I said, "is a very fast mirror."

- It reflects our objectives.
- It amplifies our incentives.
- It accelerates our decisions.

Researchers had already warned that AI in finance could stabilize small things while creating new systemic vulnerabilities—hidden interdependencies, model herding, sudden shifts when many systems update at once.

If you tell a thousand AI systems: "Protect me from losses. Respond quickly to stress. Cut risk when things start to look like 2008, 2010, or 2020."…they will do exactly that. And if everyone gives similar instructions, those systems will—quite rationally—stampede in the same direction. That's not evil. That's obedience… at scale.

From the WPBS perspective, the real issue wasn't that the machines flinched. It was that we had built a world where:

- a huge share of wealth was tied to continuous market functioning,

- the underlying debt and shadow structures were already stretched,
- and ordinary people had been sold products whose real risk they never saw.

The machines didn't create that world. They just made its consequences arrive faster.

Crash Week, Chapter 1, ends with the machines blinking first. In the next chapter, the humans finally panic:

- Central banks dust off the emergency playbooks,
- politicians scramble to assign blame and promise salvation,
- and the question hangs in the air: "If we bail this out again, who are we saving—the system, or the story?"

And in the middle of that storm, WPBS investors—bleakly realistic about the damage, quietly optimistic about their preparation—begin to do the thing this whole book is really about: Using chaos not just to protect themselves, but to buy and build the next world on behalf of their communities.

Chapter 9

The Bailout That Couldn't Fix the Story

By mid-week, the crash had moved from finance news to family group chats. That's when you know it's real. Aunties who had never once mentioned the S&P 500 were forwarding memes about "The Great Reset." Uncles who still called every crypto "Bitcoin" were asking if they should "go to cash," as if that word still meant what they thought it meant. On the screens, red numbers. On the streets, regular life—for now.

In the boardrooms and cabinet rooms, though, people were having very old conversations with very new vocabulary. Because when the machines flinch first (Chapter 8), sooner or later humans have to pick a side:

- Do we let this burn?
- Do we try to save it?
- Who do we save if we save it?

And that's where 2029 ran headfirst into its own history.

We'd Done This Before

This wasn't the first time the world improvised a bailout on live TV. In 2008, when Lehman Brothers collapsed and the global interbank market began freezing, central banks and governments responded with a flood of extraordinary measures:

- expanding emergency lending,
- guaranteeing certain bank liabilities,

- injecting capital into failing institutions,
- and unleashing large-scale asset purchase programs ("quantitative easing") to stabilize markets.

The IMF and central bank post-mortems later noted that these interventions, combined with fiscal stimulus, helped prevent a full-scale depression—but also sparked intense debates about moral hazard, inequality, and the political legitimacy of saving Wall Street while households suffered. In March 2020, when the pandemic shutdown triggered the "dash for cash," central banks again acted as dealers of last resort:

- the U.S. Federal Reserve rolled out massive facilities to support Treasury markets, corporate bonds, money market funds, and even municipal bonds, alongside trillions in QE and emergency lending;
- other major central banks launched or expanded their own purchase programs and liquidity lines.

These moves successfully calmed acute market stress—but once again raised criticism that financial markets received rapid, targeted support while fiscal help for households and small businesses was slower and more uneven.

By the early 2020s, analysts were already warning that markets had become addicted to the assumption that central banks would step in whenever asset prices fell too far, too fast—the so-called "central bank put."

So in 2029, when prices tumbled, everyone knew the pattern:

1. Market breaks.
2. Central banks talk.
3. Central banks act.
4. Markets (usually) cheer.

Only this time, something was different:

- Inflation scars from the early 2020s were still fresh.
- Debt levels—sovereign, corporate, household—were higher and more sensitive to rates.
- Trust in institutions (Chapter 2) was near historic lows.

The tools were familiar. The politics of using them had changed.

The Emergency Zoom of Planet Earth

On Day 3 of Crash Week, every serious financial official on Earth seemed to be on the same giant, laggy video call. Of course, officially, they weren't. There were separate G20 calls, regional calls, bilateral calls. But if you could have stacked them into one screen, you'd have seen:

- sleep-deprived central bankers staring at charts of funding markets,
- finance ministers staring at bond yields,
- supervisors staring at dashboards of vulnerable banks and funds.

They all had the same questions:

- Are funding markets seizing up?
- Are key institutions at risk of failing in a disorderly way?
- Are we seeing bank runs, or just non-bank runs?
- If we intervene, can we do it in a way that looks like "supporting the system," not "bailing out the rich again"?

They had fresh homework to reference:

- IMF reports warning that, although near-term risks appeared contained in some years, medium-term vulnerabilities from high public and private debt, stretched asset valuations, and non-bank leverage were serious.

- FSB and BIS work documenting how non-bank financial intermediaries—money funds, bond funds, hedge funds, private credit—could transmit and amplify shocks, and urging reforms that were only partially implemented.
- Newer analyses about stablecoins and tokenised assets posing potential threats to financial stability if widely used and poorly regulated.

Everybody had read the PDFs. Now they had to choose which page of which report to live out.

"We Stand Ready" - The Greatest Hits Tour

The first official statements were comfort food for markets:

- "Our banking system remains well-capitalized and resilient."
- "We are monitoring market developments closely."
- "We stand ready to use our full range of tools to support the smooth functioning of markets and the flow of credit to households and businesses."

Behind that smooth language were some very specific levers:

1. Liquidity Facilities for Banks - Central banks could expand discount windows, term funding programs, and swap lines—building on tools used in 2008, 2011, and 2020—to ensure banks had access to cheap funding against good collateral.

2. Backstops for Key Markets - If government bond markets or commercial paper markets seized up, they could revive or expand asset purchase programs and emergency facilities, as they had in the Treasury and corporate bond markets during the pandemic.

3. Targeted Support for Non-Banks - With some political courage (and legal creativity), they could deploy central bank or Treasury-backed vehicles to support money market funds, repo, and even parts of the non-bank system—again, like 2008 and 2020, but adapted to new structures.
4. Swap Lines Across Borders - Dollar liquidity swaps with other central banks—which proved crucial in previous global stresses—could be expanded to calm offshore funding markets.

There was even chatter in think-tank circles—some public, some not—about whether central banks should consider backstopping certain systemic stablecoins or issuing emergency CBDC "bridge tools" if digital payment rails seized up. IMF and FSB documents had already floated scenarios where stablecoins, if widely used for payments, might warrant special attention in crisis frameworks. In other words: The old menu, with new garnish.

The Political Hangover

There was just one problem. People were tired. After 2008, many citizens concluded—fairly or unfairly—that governments had been faster and more generous in rescuing financial institutions than in rescuing families. After 2020, they watched asset prices roar back—helped by ultra-loose monetary policy—even as many households struggled with job losses, health shocks, and uneven access to support. Studies and commentary noted how pandemic-era asset price gains disproportionately benefited wealthier households that already owned more financial assets.

By the late 2020s, trust surveys and political analysis painted a clear picture:

- deep dissatisfaction with inequality,
- broad skepticism about elites and institutions,
- and fatigue with what many saw as "bailout capitalism"—downside risk socialized, upside gains privatized.

So when rumors started that "they're about to bail out the markets again," the pushback was instant:

- Opposition politicians framed potential interventions as "another rescue for speculators."
- Activists demanded that any support package be tied to debt relief, wage protections, and direct help to households—not just to investors and institutions.
- Commentators pointed out that public debt levels were already high, and warned about repeating large-scale QE in a world still scarred by recent inflation episodes.

Central bank independence, once a dry academic topic, suddenly looked fragile. If your job is price stability and financial stability, what do you do when the tools for one seem to endanger the other? Cut rates and restart asset purchases aggressively, and critics will say you're reigniting inflation and bailing out asset owners. Do nothing, and critics will say you're letting a preventable financial crisis crush the real economy. In that no-win scenario, most of the key players did what humans always do when caught between bad options: They tried to split the difference.

The Half-Bailout

The crash response of 2029 will go down in history books as the Half-Bailout:

- Big enough to keep the pipes from freezing solid.
- Not big enough to keep everybody happy.
- Carefully targeted—on paper—to "market functioning" rather than "asset prices."

Concretely, it looked like this:

1. Funding Backstops, Not Blankets - Central banks offered generous term funding to banks and certain non-banks against high-quality collateral, but avoided broad new QE at first. The official line emphasized support for "market functioning" rather than "stimulating demand."
2. Stabilizing "Plumbing" Markets - Facilities for government bonds, repos, and key short-term funding instruments were reactivated or expanded, echoing the 2008 and 2020 playbooks but with stricter conditions.
3. No Direct Stablecoin Backstop (At First) - Rather than explicitly guaranteeing GDS or any specific stablecoin, authorities focused on ensuring the stability of the underlying assets—T-bills, deposits, and money-like instruments—and pushed issuers to improve transparency, risk buffers, and redemption arrangements under close supervision.
4. Macroprudential Tightrope - Supervisors leaned on banks and large non-banks to conserve capital, limit payouts, and strengthen liquidity, but tried to avoid outright credit crunches by encouraging continued lending to the real economy.
5. Political Sweeteners - In some countries, any crisis support package came bundled with symbolic and real concessions:
    - temporary relief on certain household debts,
    - targeted support for small businesses,
    - commitments to investigate "excessive risk-taking" in the non-bank sector.

It was, in short, an attempt to say: "We will stop the bleeding in the pipes without giving Wall Street another champagne IV." Markets, being markets, heard something slightly different: "They're stepping in… but they're also scared… and they're not going as big as last time… yet." So the acute freefall slowed. But the mood did not flip to euphoria. Instead, it shifted to a tense, grinding volatility.

The Story That Finally Broke

Historically, major crises don't just break balance sheets.

They break stories.

- 1970s stagflation broke the story of "We can always trade a bit more inflation for a bit more employment."
- 1990s Asian and Russian crises broke the story of "Emerging markets are a one-way convergence trade."
- 2008 broke the story of "Sophisticated finance has banished old-fashioned bank runs."
- 2020 broke the story of "Pandemics are a thing of the past in rich countries."

The 2029 crash broke this story: "If things get really bad, grown-ups will hit the big red button and make it all go back to normal."

Because while the Half-Bailout stopped a full systemic seizure, it did not restore the old normal:

- Asset prices did not V-shape right back to highs.
- Several funds and non-bank institutions failed or restructured in messy ways.
- GDS eventually re-pegged closer to $1, but with scars on its reputation and tighter, more intrusive regulation.
- Cash-plus-style products survived in some forms but lost their aura of "almost cash."

Most importantly:

- People who had thought of markets as a slightly bumpy escalator up discovered that the escalator could reverse and leave you on the floor.
- People who had relied on "central bank puts" learned that there are political and economic limits to how often and how powerfully that put can be exercised.

The system survived—but the myth of permanent rescue did not.

From a WPBS angle, that was painful for many… and clarifying for us.

What WPBS Did While the World Refreshed the Ticker

In the church basement, we didn't celebrate the crisis. We weren't rooting for anybody's 401(k) to evaporate. But we had spent years preaching—and acting on—a simple belief "Storms are inevitable. Preparation is not a luxury. Community is not optional." So while the big players argued over who should get what slice of emergency support, WPBS investors quietly executed the playbook we'd rehearsed.

1. We Didn't Have to Sell - Because we had insisted on:
    - meaningful cash and T-bill buffers,
    - low leverage,
    - and portfolios sized to our real risk tolerance, we weren't forced into liquidation at the worst prices.

That alone separated us from millions who discovered, too late, that they were "long the bull market" with borrowed money.

2. We Bought What Still Made Sense - Not everything crashing is on sale. Some things are just garbage falling back to Earth. But some assets—especially local, real-economy ones—got marked down for no fundamental reason:

- viable small businesses starved of credit,
- community properties whose financing got temporarily messy,
- essential-service infrastructure facing short-term funding gaps.

Because we weren't overextended, WPBS entities could step in as buy-and-hold rescuers—acquiring stakes, refinancing on fair terms, or co-owning critical assets with community partners.

3. We Strengthened Internal Safety Nets - Crash Week exposed who in our communities were most vulnerable:

    - people living paycheck to paycheck whose employers were already talking layoffs,
    - elders whose retirement accounts took sudden hits,
    - small landlords and tenants caught between mortgages and rent.

So while the news obsessed over the next basis point in bond yields, we:

- topped up mutual aid funds,
- extended no-interest emergency loans in some cases,
- pressed pause on certain distributions to build resilience before returns.

4. We Told the Truth—Gently, But Clearly

In sermons, study groups, and coaching calls, we said out loud what many felt:

- No, they cannot completely bail out everything, every time."
- "Yes, some of this pain comes from years of decisions made far above your pay grade."
- "And yes, some of our own habits—over-consumption,

under-saving, blind trust in 'safe' products—left us more exposed than we needed to be."

5. But we wrapped that truth in hope:
    - Hope rooted in God, not the S&P.
    - Hope expressed in concrete steps, not vague "thoughts and prayers."
    - Hope that said, "We can build something more just, more resilient, more community-owned on the other side of this."
6. We Took Notes
   Crash Week was not just an event; it was data.
   For a movement like WPBS, the question was:
   "What did we get right?
   Where were we still too dependent on fragile systems?
   Which of our people suffered the most, and why?
   How do we adjust the blueprint so the next storm finds us even stronger?"
7. We saw firsthand:
    - which banks actually honored their commitments;
    - which platforms stayed up under stress;
    - which local leaders showed up for their people;
    - which investments aligned with our mission and which were just shiny. And we updated our designs accordingly.

Bleak for the System, Bright for the Builders

From one angle, the post-crash landscape looked bleak:

- The global financial system survived, but trust took another hit.

- Non-bank regulation had to tighten, which meant less cheap, sloppy credit flowing to easy-money schemes.
- The AI hype cycle deflated from "redefine everything tomorrow" to "transform some things, disrupt others, disappoint many."
- Sovereigns that were already stretched found it harder to borrow cheaply, forcing painful choices about spending and reform.

Growth projections were revised down. Debt-service projections were revised up.

Geopolitical tensions sharpened. Not exactly the stuff of feel-good investor brochures. But from another angle, for WPBS-style investors, the horizon looked… honest. Because we had never built our hope on:

- permanently rising valuations,
- permanently calm spreads,
- permanently generous central banks.

We had built it on:

- real assets serving real needs,
- community ownership and cooperation,
- barbell strategies that assumed chaos is not the exception but the environment.

In that world:

- A system that can no longer paper over its contradictions with free money is painful—but truthful.
- A market that finally prices risk more soberly is dangerous—but fairer to the prepared.
- A society that has to stop pretending "everything is fine" is frightening—but open to new narratives.

The 2029 crash, then, was both:

- a judgment on decades of wishful thinking and unequal rescue, and
- an opportunity for communities like ours to step out of mere survival and into shaping the next regime.

As Chapter 9 closes, the Half-Bailout has done its work:

- The bleeding has slowed.
- The headlines have downgraded from "historic collapse" to "continuing uncertainty."
- The loudest panic has given way to a quieter, grinding anxiety.

Markets are no longer falling off a cliff. They are rearranging themselves.

And in that in-between—after the old story breaks but before a new one is universally agreed upon— that is where WPBS was always meant to stand:

- not as spectators,
- not as opportunistic vultures,
- but as builders carrying a blueprint.

In the next chapter, we leave the macro lens and zoom in: We follow specific WPBS investors—teachers, veterans, nurses, small business owners—as they make concrete moves in the rubble of 2029:

- what they buy,
- what they build,
- what they forgive,
- and how they quietly begin to answer the question the crash left hanging:

"If the old system can't keep its promises… what new promises are we, together, brave enough to make—and keep?"

2029

Chapter 10

Blueprints in the Rubble

The Markets Stopped Screaming Before The People Did

By the second week after Crash Week, the indices had downgraded from "demonic shriek" to "chronic cough." The tickers still wobbled. The commentators still tried to explain yesterday with last year's clichés. The central bankers still appeared on screens, looking like they hadn't slept since the Clinton administration. But on regular streets, the crisis had turned into something quieter and more dangerous:

- HR emails with phrases like "strategic restructuring."
- Quiet "For Lease" signs in shop windows.
- City budget meetings with a lot of sighing.
- That look in people's eyes that says,

"Whatever that was… I'm not sure anyone is really driving this bus."

The Half-Bailout (Chapter 9) had kept the pipes from freezing. But it could not make the water taste like trust again. That's where WPBS stepped out of the abstract.

Up to this point, "West Philadelphia Billionaires Society" sounded like a glorious, slightly ridiculous phrase spoken in a church basement over bad coffee and good vision.

Now it was about to be:

- a laundromat,
- a clinic,
- a corner store,
- a block of houses,

- a local loan fund
- and a handful of ordinary saints holding blueprints over rubble.

The Unlikely Board Meeting

It started, as most revolutions do, with folding chairs. In the KCC fellowship hall, a small knot of early WPBS participants gathered around a borrowed projector. The market was still jittery. Phones still buzzed with "urgent updates." Yet here they sat, not trading, not doom-scrolling, but planning.

- Renee, night-shift nurse, small-time investor, large-time prayer warrior.
- Malik, bus driver, side-hustle mechanic, numbers nerd on the low.
- Miss Laverne, retired teacher, human filing cabinet of everybody's business, and unofficial historian.
- Jay, Army vet with a disability rating, a toolbox, and a loud laugh that came from somewhere deeper than jokes.

They were not Wall Street. They were not Silicon Valley. They were not Davos. They were the exact people the old system treated as "end-users" of whatever someone else decided. Except now, they had receipts:

- A crash that proved "safe-ish" funds weren't safe.
- A stablecoin wobble that proved "programmable money" wasn't magic.
- A Half-Bailout that proved the cavalry had limits.

On the screen behind them, a simple slide:

WPBS POST-CRASH PLAYBOOK

Assets down. Trust down. Rents still due. What do we buy? What do we build? What do we forgive? No hype. No fireworks. Just a decision: "If the big story is broken, our little stories have to get serious."

Remembering Who Has Done This Before

Before they talked about what to do, they reminded themselves what had been done—by others, in other times, with less tech and less noise. Miss Laverne, of course, had the receipts. She pulled up an article on the Mondragon Corporation in Spain: a federation of worker cooperatives that grew from a small technical college project in the 1950s into a group with tens of thousands of worker-owners across finance, industry, retail, and education. Worker-owners, not outside shareholders. Executive pay capped relative to the lowest worker. Profits reinvested in jobs and community, not just stock buybacks. She clicked over to the "Cleveland Model" and the Evergreen Cooperatives: anchor-backed worker co-ops in one of America's poorest cities, created specifically to hire people facing barriers to employment and build community wealth, with local hospitals and universities committing some of their massive purchasing power to buy from them. Then she showed the story of the Dudley Street Neighborhood Initiative in Boston: a resident-led organization in a disinvested neighborhood that organized so powerfully the city gave them eminent domain over vacant land, allowing them to create a community land trust so the community itself could permanently control land use and affordability.

And because history in Black communities always comes with both glory and grief, they spent a minute on Tulsa's Greenwood District:

- In 1921, "Black Wall Street"—a thriving Black community with over a hundred Black-owned businesses, professionals, and skilled craftspeople—was destroyed in a coordinated racist massacre.

- Recent Department of Justice reports have finally acknowledged the organized nature of the attack and official complicity, and Tulsa's city government has only now, more than a century later, begun offering reparations packages for housing, historic preservation, and business support.

Greenwood was proof of two things at once:

1. Black communities can build serious wealth and infrastructure.
2. The system will sometimes burn it down rather than share power.

Renee shook her head.

So Mondragon shows we can run multibillion-euro co-ops. Cleveland shows we can harness anchor money for co-ops. Dudley Street shows we can own the land. Greenwood shows we've already done Black Wall Street once… and what happens when we have prosperity without enough protection.

She looked around the room. "WPBS is not a brand-new dream. It's a remix."

The Three Buckets: Buy, Build, Bank

The crash had knocked asset prices down. But it had also knocked clarity up. WPBS simplified its post-crash strategy into three buckets:

1. BUY – Acquire existing assets the community needed, at distressed prices when possible.
2. BUILD – Start or expand cooperative, community-owned enterprises where there were gaps.
3. BANK – Strengthen community-controlled finance—credit unions, CDFI-like funds—to reduce dependence on fragile, extractive lenders.

They used real-world models as their receipts:

- Community development financial institutions (CDFIs)—certified banks, credit unions, loan funds, and VC funds with an explicit mission to bring capital to underserved communities, supported by the U.S. CDFI Fund.
- Community land trusts (CLTs)—nonprofits that own land for community benefit, taking it off the speculative market and keeping housing and commercial space permanently affordable.

WPBS didn't need to invent everything from scratch. It just needed to stack these proven tools into one coherent Black-and-brown–centered blueprint.

Case Study #1: The Laundromat That Turned Into a Bank Account

On 52nd Street, a family-run laundromat was gasping. Rising utilities. A landlord itching to raise rent or sell the building. Customers squeezed by the crash. The owner, Mr. Ortiz, confided in Renee: "If this keeps up, I'll have to sell. Maybe to one of those chains. They said they'd turn it into 'Luxury Wash Experience.' I don't even know what that means."

WPBS had a rule:

If a neighborhood essential is about to become a soulless franchise—or vanish—that's a siren.

The crew ran the numbers:

- Laundry is a recession-resistant business; clothes still get dirty.
- The books were messy but salvageable.
- The building, if they could get it, sat on a corner that would only get more valuable.

They pulled from all three buckets:

- A WPBS investment club bought a majority stake in the business, with Mr. Ortiz retaining a meaningful share and operational leadership.
- They negotiated with a mission-focused lender—a local credit union with CDFI certification—to refinance the building debt on fairer terms, using the laundromat cash flow as part of the case.
- They wrote into the operating agreement that staff could become worker-owners over time, Mondragon-style, with profit-sharing and governance rights as tenure milestones.

They added one more twist: A small "community dividend" line in the pro forma—5% of net profits set aside for:

- emergency rent relief,
- youth stipends for neighborhood clean-ups,
- and a tiny seed pot for the next micro-business.

Was this going to make anyone a billionaire overnight? No. But it turned a soon-to-be-lost neighborhood asset into:

- a multi-owner, cross-generational business,
- a small local employer with an ownership path,
- and a micro–community endowment in disguise.

Renee joked: "We basically turned washers and dryers into a savings account with spin cycle." Nobody laughed at the pun. They were too busy taking notes.

Case Study #2: From Abandoned Lots to "Don't Sell Grandma's House"

Out near the trolley line, there was a block that looked like a before picture:

- Two boarded-up rowhouses.
- Three vacant lots used as unofficial parking and very official dumping.
- A tired corner store selling more lotto than lettuce.

Property values had dipped in the crash, but speculative interest… had not. Developers were circling like buzzards with spreadsheets. WPBS had studied Dudley Street and its community land trust, which used legal tools and community organizing to gain control over dozens of acres in Boston's Roxbury and North Dorchester neighborhoods, keeping land for permanently affordable housing and community uses.

The team in West Philly knew they didn't yet have Dudley's level of power—no eminent domain, not enough capital. But they had: relationships, a crash discount, and a clear sense of what would happen if they did nothing. So they did something small but decisive:

1. Formed a Mini-CLT

   They established a local nonprofit land trust, aligned with WPBS principles, with a clear charter:

   - acquire land in the neighborhood;
   - keep it out of speculative flipping;
   - lease it to community members and co-ops at stable, affordable rates.

2. Bought One House and One Lot

   No grand slam—just enough to:

   - renovate one rowhouse for mixed-income tenants,
   - turn one vacant lot into a small green space and community garden.

3. Attached a Rule: "Don't Sell Grandma's House"

   The CLT model kept the land in trust permanently.

   Homeowners could build equity in the structure but not sell the land to the highest bidder, keeping prices more stable for future generations and preserving community control.

   They pitched it this way: "This is not charity. This is us deciding that our grandkids will not have to drive through here saying, 'My grandma used to live there before it was condos.'" Mondragon proved industrial co-ops could anchor a region. Dudley Street proved a community could anchor land permanently. WPBS decided an Afro-diasporic neighborhood could do both—slowly, one block at a time.

Case Study #3: The Little Fund That Saw People, Not Risk

As the crash's second and third waves rolled through, people who had never missed a payment in their lives suddenly needed, bridge money between jobs, cash to keep a tiny business open, funds to cover surprise medical costs. Mainstream lenders responded the way they always do, tighter standards, higher rates for the "risky," cheery ads about "We're here to help" with footnotes that said, "But probably not you."

WPBS had been watching CDFIs for years: mission-driven banks, credit unions, and loan funds explicitly created to bring capital to communities mainstream finance tends to label "too risky," backed and certified by the U.S. CDFI Fund. These institutions had already, financed small businesses in disinvested areas, funded affordable housing, provided credit and financial services where big banks had closed branches.

So the question for WPBS wasn't "Can it be done?" The question was, "How much of this can we own?" They started with a micro-version, pooled contributions—$10, $25, $50 at a time—from WPBS participants, matched a portion with a local CDFI partner created a micro-loan fund underwritten not only by credit scores but by community knowledge.

Deacon Malik explained the underwriting model: "The credit report don't show who's been taking care of folks for twenty years. We know who's solid. We live next door."

The loans were small:

- $2,000 to keep a food truck's engine running.
- $1,500 to cover a certification course leading to a better-paying job.
- $3,000 for emergency roof repairs that kept a house habitable and a family stable.

But the signal was big: "We are not just consumers of capital. We are issuers of mercy and money—with terms." Over time, the plan was to formalize the fund, seek official CDFI certification or partnership, leverage matching capital from larger programs, and eventually act as an on-ramp to larger cooperative projects. But even at this humble stage, it was already doing what many CDFIs do nationally. Seeing opportunity where big finance only sees risk.

Humor as a Survival Strategy

Through all this, the jokes never stopped. When someone asked whether WPBS was "trying to become the Black Mondragon," Jay said: "No, Mondragon is trying to be the Spanish WPBS; they just started earlier."

When Miss Laverne explained community land trusts and someone complained about the complexity, she answered: "Sugar, a 30-year mortgage is complex and you signed that.

Don't tell me we can't learn our own paperwork."

When the micro-loan fund's first borrower paid back early and the spreadsheet lit up green, Malik stood up like a coach after a winning touchdown: "Behold, the miracle of on-time payments in the hood. Somebody call the rating agencies!"

Humor didn't trivialize the work. It kept the work human, in a world where the big system kept trying to reduce everyone to "flows," "segments," and "risk buckets."

Beyond Survival: Toward a New Story

Here's the thing about 2029: For the old system, it was a crisis. For WPBS, it was an unscheduled launch window. The crash pushed some assets down into reach, exposed which leaders and institutions could be trusted, and convinced a whole generation that the old promises were not coming back in their childhood form. Into that vacuum stepped: laundromats becoming mini-Mondragons; land trusts turning "not my neighborhood" into "our neighborhood's land bank"; micro-funds behaving like pocket-sized CDFIs, betting on people the algorithms ignored. None of this erased the pain of 2029. None of it fixed national debt levels or geopolitical tensions. But it did something the Half-Bailout never could, It changed who held the chalk when the future of specific blocks, businesses, and families was being drawn. And under all of it, like a bass line the news couldn't hear, was memory: memory of Greenwood's brilliance and its burning; memory of Mondragon's quiet, stubborn experiment in worker power; memory of Dudley Street's insistence that a neighborhood can and must own its land; memory of CDFIs and credit unions that kept lending where big banks shut branches and moved on.

WPBS was not creating something from nothing. It was braiding: cooperative ownership, land stewardship, community finance, diasporic faith, and post-crash clarity. Bleak for the broad indices? Yes. Brutally honest about systemic limits? Absolutely. But for WPBS investors, this was the chapter where "prophetic fiction" started to feel suspiciously like minutes from last Tuesday's meeting.

As Chapter 10 closes, the camera pulls back one laundramat, one rowhouse and lot, one tiny loan fund, a handful of people with spreadsheets open and Bibles nearby, stacked against a global financial system that still believes "next quarter" is the main character.

In the next chapter, the focus widens again:

We trace how these scattered WPBS outposts—in West Philly, in Accra, in Kingston, in Lagos, in Toronto - begin to recognize each other, forming a quiet, transnational network of post-crash builders who are not waiting for the next bailout, because they have finally understood: The old story was about "too big to fail." The new story is about too rooted to uproot.

2029

Chapter 11

The Diaspora Mesh

The first time somebody called it "The Diaspora Mesh," it was a joke in a WhatsApp group.

It stuck because it was accidentally true.

By late 2029, the WPBS idea had leaked way beyond West Philly—like curry smell in an apartment building, or gossip in a Black beauty shop. Quiet at first, then sudden. One minute, it was just a book and a basement. The next minute, screenshots were hopping time zones faster than anybody's 401(k) could recover. And the timing was suspicious. Because while the official experts were obsessing over bond spreads and AI risk models, something else was happening under their feet: The African Diaspora, Caribbean Diaspora, and Afro-descended communities worldwide were already moving hundreds of billions of dollars a year… one little remittance at a time. The crash hadn't stopped that flow. If anything, it had focused it.

The River Nobody Controlled

For decades, economists had called remittances "private flows" in their PowerPoints—money migrants send back home to support family, pay school fees, fix the roof after a storm, or keep a little shop alive. By 2024, officially recorded remittances to low- and middle-income countries were estimated around $685 billion—larger than foreign aid and often more stable than foreign investment.

- Sub-Saharan Africa alone was receiving on the order of $90–100 billion a year, and those flows had roughly doubled over the previous decade.

- Latin America and the Caribbean were pulling in over $150–160 billion annually, much of it from migrants in the United States and Europe sending money back to small islands and hillside towns.
- The world argued about aid packages, debt relief, and IMF conditions.

Meanwhile, aunties, uncles, cousins, and "that boy who left in 2015" were quietly sending more money home than most governments. No parliamentary vote. No press conference. Just "Sent ✅" on a phone screen. Security analysts called remittances a "risk factor." God called them "I see you taking care of your people."

How a Book Became a Side Quest in the Remittance Economy

Somebody in Toronto bought "2029: The Post-MAGA Global Financial Market Crash" on a whim. They finished it in two nights, underlining half of it and side-eyeing their own TFSA. They passed it to a cousin in London, who passed it to a sister in Accra, who passed it to a brother in Lagos, who dropped it in a family WhatsApp group where, frankly, nobody had time for a 300-page economic prophecy… until the screenshots started landing with the words: "This is literally what we're living. Also, this man keeps saying 'one million of your closest friends.'" It hit differently outside the U.S.

Because for them, the crash wasn't just about Wall Street valuations. It was about: exchange rates suddenly making tuition and medicine more expensive, job cuts in host countries where immigrants were always first on the chopping block, governments back home quietly counting on remittances to plug budget holes long before any "aid" arrived.

In Accra, one young woman said it out loud on a late-night call: "If we are already sending billions home, and they are already blocking and crashing and confiscating at the top… why can't we be the WPBS? Not just West Philly. West Planet Billionaires Society." That was the night the Diaspora Mesh got its name.

Mesh Node #1: Accra - "From Mobile Money to Local Power"

Ghana's capital had been on the front lines of digital finance for years: Mobile money adoption had exploded across Africa, letting people send and receive funds on basic phones. Fintech startups chasing lower-cost digital remittances were popping up, promising to beat the old-school transfer giants on fees and speed.

In one little co-working space, a tiny group of WPBS readers—a software engineer, a nurse just back from the U.K., a university lecturer, and a taxi driver with a hustler's eye—sat around a plastic table. They pulled up the data:

- Africa's remittances had climbed toward $95–100+ billion by the mid-2020s, becoming one of the continent's largest and most stable sources of external finance.

The engineer did some quick math: "If even 1% of that—just one out of every hundred dollars—was routed into community-owned co-ops, land trusts, and credit unions instead of disappearing into fees and rent? That's a billion dollars a year of patient capital."

The nurse snorted. "One percent is just the part Western Union normally eats for lunch."They weren't naïve. They knew: families needed remittances now for food, rent, school fees; governments were starting to see diaspora money as a development strategy and even a line item in national planning; if they tried to "redirect" too much too fast, they'd trigger resistance from the very people they wanted to help. So they started with something small and almost boring: A Diaspora Mesh Wallet pilot.

- Aunties and uncles abroad who were already sending money home were invited to round up transfers by a few dollars.
- Those extra dollars went into a separately tracked wallet, governed by a small community board, earmarked for cooperative projects—not emergency consumption.

First use case? A community-owned cold storage and distribution co-op linking small farmers outside Accra to urban markets, modeled loosely on African agricultural cooperatives that had long played a role in marketing produce, providing inputs, and pooling risk.

- Diaspora Mesh money helped fund the refrigerators.
- Local members contributed labor, land, and local knowledge.
- Profits were split among cooperative members, with a small return to the Diaspora Mesh pool—not Wall Street.

Nobody on CNBC cared. But a grandmother in Kumasi noticed she could buy vegetables that stayed fresh longer. That was enough.

Mesh Node #2: Kingston - "From Barrel Economy to Block Economy"

In Jamaica, everybody knows barrels. The ones packed in foreign basements with rice, flour, clothes, and snacks, then shipped home like floating care packages. By the mid-2020s, remittances to Latin America and the Caribbean were soaring—more than $150 billion a year—supporting households, small businesses, and community survival in ways formal "development" often ignored. In a church hall in Kingston, a WPBS reading circle met between services.

They had all seen the headlines about aid rows, debt negotiations, and new geopolitical games in the Caribbean. They'd also seen commentary pointing out that U.S. aid and big-power generosity had often been instruments of control, and that crises could be opportunities for the region to pursue economic independence and deeper regional cooperation. They asked a sharp, impolite question: "If they can cut aid when they feel like it, but they cannot stop me Western Unioning money to my auntie, then where is the real power line?"

They decided to answer it with: one neighborhood, one block, one experiment.

They called it Barrel to Block.

Instead of just sending barrels and cash that disappeared into individual survival, a small group of diaspora relatives agreed to:

- keep doing that for necessities;
- but also, once a quarter, send a modest extra amount to a Block Fund run by trusted local stewards.

The Block Fund's rules were simple:

1. Money goes into revenue-producing, community-owned assets on this block—shops, solar micro-grids, rental units, small manufacturing.
2. Ownership is structured as a co-op or land-trust hybrid: the land/property is held in a nonprofit trust to keep it from speculative flipping, while local residents buy shares in the buildings or businesses over time.
3. Diaspora contributors don't just "donate." They hold patient, capped-return shares, with a portion of returns reserved for community projects and a portion recycled to seed the next block.

It wasn't perfect. There were arguments, missteps, and at least one cousin who thought this was a scam until he saw the first micro-solar grid lowering his mother's light bill. But over a few years, something shifted:

- That one block had fewer "For Sale to Developers" signs.
- Several young people who had been planning to leave started small ventures right there—because rent and power costs were stable enough to plan around.
- The diaspora relatives stopped seeing their remittances as money thrown down a sinkhole and started calling them "investments in land we don't intend to lose twice."

Somebody drew it on a napkin: "Barrel economy" = stuff goes in, disappears "Block economy" = stuff goes in, multiplies, stays The math wasn't magic. It was just cooperative economics with better group chats.

Mesh Node #3: Lagos – "When the Hustle Meets the Heritage"

Lagos had always been a place where hustle and chaos did the tango. By the late 2020s, it was also a major node in Africa's digital and fintech boom, with startups building everything from payment rails to cross-border remittance pipes. A small WPBS circle there had two obsessions:

1. How to cut remittance costs for families.
2. How to recycle some of that money into African-owned infrastructure instead of foreign-owned apps.

They had read up on the long history of cooperatives among the African diaspora and on the continent itself; farmer co-ops pooling resources and marketing crops, savings clubs and rotating credit associations, Black co-ops in the Americas forming grocery stores, insurance funds, and mutual aid societies when mainstream institutions shut them out. They also knew the dangers of over-relying on any one digital platform, especially in a world where regulations, sanctions, and corporate mergers could make your favorite app disappear overnight. So they built a two-layered Mesh:

- Layer 1: Payment Rails – Work with existing digital remittance startups to negotiate lower fees and better terms for Mesh participants, aggregating volume to get leverage.
- Layer 2: Ownership Pool – Skim a small, transparent fee on top of Mesh remittances—not to enrich the app, but to build an African-owned co-investment fund focused on energy, logistics, and data infrastructure.

Think of it as: "We'll use your pipes. But we're not going to stop there. We are also going to buy our own pipes."

Over time, the Lagos node started co-investing tiny slices of that pooled capital into: a local solar mini-grid co-op in a peri-urban community, an equity stake in a logistics platform that hired from and served under-resourced neighborhoods, and shared-ownership data centers that hosted African content and services. It wasn't glamorous. There were no Super Bowl ads. But every time the old system flinched—every time a global crash, a sanctions regime, or a new regulation made traditional capital run scared—those tiny co-owned assets kept humming. Not because they were invincible. Because they were needed.

Mesh Node #4: Toronto / London / Philly - "The Credit Union Chronicles"

The other side of the Mesh lived where the remittances started. In North America and Europe, Black communities had a long record of building their own financial institutions:

- Black-owned banks dating back to the late 19th century, created because mainstream banks would not lend to Black households and businesses.
- Black credit unions and savings co-ops organized through churches and mutual aid societies, especially in the early 20th century and again during the civil rights era.

Researchers and movement historians had documented how these cooperatives and minority-owned CDFIs brought capital and services to communities redlined out of mainstream finance, often making smaller, more tailored loans than large banks considered "worth their time."

WPBS readers in Toronto and London saw this and asked:

"If our people here are already using Black-owned banks and credit unions, and our people there are receiving remittances, why isn't the line between them ours?"

In Toronto:

- A small Black-led credit union piloted a "Diaspora Mesh Account" product:
    - customers could auto-allocate a percentage of their deposits to:
    - local community investments (co-ops, affordable housing, small business loans), and
    - diaspora Mesh projects vetted by partner co-ops in Africa and the Caribbean.
    - the credit union partnered with existing CDFIs and minority-owned institutions to share risk and know-how.

In London:

- A Black-run investment club, inspired by both WPBS and classic "susu" rotating savings groups, formalized as a cooperative society that:
    - contributed capital to Black-owned banks and CDFIs abroad;
    - participated in secondary capital programs that strengthened their balance sheets, increasing lending capacity to communities back home.

In Philly:

- Folks who had already been in the KCC basement from the beginning started:
    - shifting more of their own deposits into Black-owned banks and credit unions;
    - buying small stakes in new institutions like Redemption Bank in the Rockies, part of a newer wave of Black-owned, tech-forward banks aiming to serve communities nationwide via digital platforms.

They joked: "If we're going to be sending money over oceans anyway, the river at least needs to flow through our hands twice."

Humor, Holy Ghost, and High-Speed Rails

It would be a lie to say everyone understood the Mesh. Some folks just wanted to know: "Will this lower my fees? Will Grandma get her money faster? Will it stop the bank from doing that thing where they smile and still decline you?" Others rolled their eyes: "Y'all trying to be United Nations with prayer hands." So the Mesh kept its theology and its spreadsheets simple:

- Theology:

  "We are stewards, not spectators. The earth is the Lord's, but this block is our assignment."

- Spreadsheets:

  "We track:
    - how much went out as remittances;
    - how much was skimmed (with consent!) for collective investment;
    - what assets and institutions that capital bought;
    - and how many families those assets served."

Underneath the jokes was a sobering understanding:

- Remittances were already bigger than foreign aid in many regions.
- Cooperatives and credit unions had always been Black people's quiet counter-strategy to exclusion and predatory finance.
- CDFIs and Black-owned banks were uniquely positioned to serve communities mainstream markets called "too risky"—and to keep doing so in crisis.

The crash didn't invent the Mesh. It just made it obvious.

The workflows had always been there:

- Aunt in New York → MoneyGram → Grocery shop in St. Mary.
- Cousin in London → Bank wire → School fees in Kumasi.
- Brother in Philly → CashApp → Rent money in Lagos.

All WPBS did was ask:"What if 1–5% of that river became a permanent community reservoir, instead of just passing through?" And then do the boring, sacred work of: forming co-ops, land trusts, credit unions, and funds; negotiating with regulators and platforms; and keeping receipts so the Mesh didn't become a vibe without a balance sheet.

Too Rooted to Uproot

By the early 2030s, if you zoomed way out, the world still looked messy:

- Global growth was slower.
- Some governments teetered under debt burdens.
- New AI-driven markets rose and fell with dizzying speed.

- Geopolitics kept throwing plot twists no novelist would dare.

But if you zoomed in, something else was true:

- More land sat inside community land trusts, especially in neighborhoods the old system once treated as disposable.
- More businesses that survived the crash were co-owned by workers and residents who had weathered it together, not by distant shareholders who barely knew the postal code.
- More banks and credit unions explicitly serving Black and Brown communities were strengthened by intentional deposits, secondary capital, and Mesh flows.

And the remittance river? It still flowed—$100 here, $300 there, $75 when times were tight, $1,000 when things went well.

But now, alongside the individual lifelines, there was a thin, stubborn stream feeding:

- co-op laundromats and clinics,
- block-level solar and water systems,
- local loan funds with mercy in their underwriting,
- and land that "our people" would not lose for the third time in a century.

From a global finance perspective, it was still tiny. From the perspective of one family, one block, one parish, one village, it was the difference between:

- being pushed around by every market cycle, or
- being rooted enough to bend without breaking.

And that was the quiet punchline of the whole book: The 2029 crash showed what was "too big to fail" in the old story. The Diaspora Mesh started to show what was too rooted to uproot in the new one.

As Chapter 11 closes, the camera has widened: from West Philly's basement to Accra's co-working space; from Kingston's barrels to Lagos's fintech offices; from Black-run credit unions in Toronto and Philly to aunties wiring rent from Birmingham and Brooklyn.

The Mesh is not a company. It's not even a single formal organization. It's a pattern: people who share blood, faith, and history quietly deciding that if they must send money across the world anyway, some of that money will come back home as power—not just as receipts.

In the next chapter, we return to where we started: Back to the basement, back to Renee and Malik and Miss Laverne and Jay, as they look up from their spreadsheets, check their texts from Ghana and Jamaica and Nigeria and Brixton, and realize that what began as a "prophetic, fictional" thought experiment has become something much more dangerous, much more holy, and much more beautiful: a global covenant of communities who have finally stopped asking the system for permission to own their tomorrow.

Chapter 12

After the Fall, Before the Billion

By the time the history books got around to 2029, they called it things like:

- "The Post-MAGA Market Regime Shift,"
- "The Great Repricing of Trust,"
- or, if the author had tenure and a sense of humor,

"That Year When Everybody Remembered Risk Was Real."

They had graphs. They had models. They had polite academic debates about "macroprudential transmission channels."

What they didn't have, not really, was you.

Not just "you the individual reader," but you plural:

- the nurse who bought a slice of the laundromat;
- the bus driver who could quote both Scripture and amortization tables;
- the auntie wiring $200 a month to Kingston and now seeing a solar grid on the block she grew up on;
- the programmer in Lagos quietly building rails for a river of diaspora money to flow through African-owned infrastructure;
- the retired teacher in West Philly who could say "Mondragon" and "community land trust" in the same breath without breaking stride.

The books called them "households," "remittance senders," "emerging market savers," "non-institutional investors." Heaven called them stewards. WPBS called them investors in the next world order, even if their portfolios looked like, 2 shares of the co-op laundromat, 0.0007% of a cold storage facility outside Accra, a few community land trust shares in Kingston, a credit union account in Philly, and a very specific corner store that would not be turned into "Luxury Wash Experience." None of that shows up in the MSCI World Index. But it shows up where it matters.

The Crisis That Refused to Waste Itself

Here's how the "serious" people eventually told the story of 2029 in conferences and reports: elevated interest rates met very high global debt; shadow banks and tokenised credit markets amplified the stress; a sequence of triggers—San Aurelio's capital controls, CashPlus gating, the GDS wobble, AI-driven de-risking—sparked a cascade; central banks deployed a Half-Bailout—funding backstops and market plumbing support without another full-blast QE; growth slumped, inequality widened (again), political anger deepened (again), and everybody promised to "do better on non-bank regulation this time."

It wasn't wrong. It just wasn't the whole truth. Because history tends to stare at the flood and miss the fact that: somebody built a higher porch, somebody dug a drainage ditch, somebody turned a flooded lot into a garden when the water receded. The 2029 crash didn't waste itself completely. Some of its wreckage became building material.

The Quiet Declaration

There was no single date you could circle on a calendar and say: "This is when WPBS became real." No IPO bell. No Davos panel. No new coin listing.

What you had instead were a thousand small declarations, none of them printed in the Financial Times:

- A pastor in Gambrills, Maryland standing in a pulpit and telling the saints,"We are not here just to survive the system. We are here to build alternatives in the Name of the One who owns the cattle on a thousand hills and the deed on this block."
- A co-op board in Philadelphia voting to adopt a hiring preference for neighborhood youth, not because it looked good on a grant application, but because they remembered what it felt like to have nowhere to be after school.
- A group of aunties in Kingston deciding that, from now on, at least one barrel per year would feed the Block Fund.
- A circle of engineers and farmers in Accra agreeing that if foreign capital wanted to co-invest in their cold storage co-op, it would be on their terms, with capped returns and local governance.
- A Black credit union board in Toronto quietly approving a new policy:

  "We will treat diaspora Mesh flows as core deposits—not hot money—because our people are not tourists in their own story."

Individually, they looked like "governance minutiae." Together, they were a verdict: "We no longer accept 'too big to fail' as the only sacred phrase in finance. Our sacred phrase is too rooted to uproot."

The Day the Graphs Got Weird

It took a while for the quants to notice. For most of the 2030s, the global charts were dominated by: a slower, more fractured world economy; multiple currency blocs; periodic flare-ups of AI-driven volatility; long arguments about climate policy and fiscal space. But then graduate students doing dissertations on "Household Wealth Dynamics in the Post-2029 Era" started seeing… anomalies. They'd filter for: Black and Brown communities in certain neighborhoods, regions with high emigration and remittance intensity, areas served by CDFIs, credit unions, and co-ops. And find: more business ownership than the models predicted, slightly higher housing stability where community land trusts existed, more resilience in income during downturns where co-ops and Mesh projects were active. Nothing dramatic. This wasn't Marvel Avengers, it was mustard seeds.

But the graphs wouldn't behave. Traditional models assumed: poorer communities = more fragile to shocks; remittance-dependent regions = permanently vulnerable "informal" finance = inherently risky and unstable. Yet in pockets where WPBS-type practices had taken root—buy, build, bank; land trust; co-op; Mesh—the data started whispering back:

"Actually… not quite. Something else is happening here." They gave it technical names:

- "Community-embedded capital formation"
- "Diaspora-cooperative feedback loops"
- "Non-state stabilization via remittance-based investment"

We just called it: "We decided to stop dying with empty hands and full receipts."

The Theology of the Ledger

If you squinted at WPBS strictly as finance, you'd miss the weirdest part: The budgets were prayed over. The meetings started with Scripture. The balance sheets were read out loud next to verses about jubilee, stewardship, and "ow[ing] no man anything, but to love one another." Not in a prosperity-gospel, "God will make your coin 10x by Friday" way. No. In a gritty, post-crash, "We will no longer bow to mammon but we will learn Excel" way.

Over time, a kind of theology of the ledger emerged:

- Every line item is a confession. Where you put money reveals what you actually believe about the future.
- Debt is not sin, but slavery is. So we avoid entanglements that would make us compromise our assignment when the next 2029 hits.
- Remittances are liturgy. They're an offering: one part survival, one part hope, one part generational stubbornness.
- Co-ops are quiet altar calls. Not just, "Will you receive Jesus?" but, "Will you receive responsibility for this block, with these people, over this time?"

You can't put that in a stress test, but you can see its fingerprints in: lower default rates in some CDFIs that underwrote character and community ties, not just credit scores; stronger loan performance in co-ops where workers were also owners; faster recovery in neighborhoods with land held in trust rather than on the speculative roller coaster. Faith didn't replace prudence. It demanded prudence

A Prophecy Fulfilled (And Still Unfolding)

Remember what the book said way back in the preface? "This is fiction, but not fantasy.

Prophetic, but not fortune-telling. A thought experiment in how a crash could go wrong—and how communities could go right."

The prophecy was never: that GDS would wobble at exactly 92 cents; that San Aurelio would be the first to slam capital controls; that CashPlus would be the exact shape of the boring fund that broke. Those details were placeholders.

The deeper prophecy was simpler:

- Systems built on denial of risk will eventually meet reality.
- Elites will try to preserve their story first, their people second.
- Crashes will come whether we are ready or not.
- Prepared, rooted communities can turn chaos into covenant.

By the time the "real" 2029 arrives in whichever timeline you're reading this from, it may not look exactly like these pages.

- Maybe the trigger is different.
- Maybe the stablecoin has another name.
- Maybe the AI panic takes a new form.

But the decision points will rhyme:

- Will we still be shocked that "safe-ish" things were not safe?
- Will we still be building lives on invisible promises we don't understand?
- Or will we have laundromats, land, loan funds, and Mesh flows already in place—small, humble, powerful?

That's the thing about prophetic fiction: It doesn't ask, "Did events match exactly?" It asks, "Did you learn anything before they did?"

The Investor Nobody Counts

Economists love counting big investors: pension funds, sovereign wealth funds, megabanks, giant asset managers. The WPBS book spends its last ink on somebody else: the Ghanaian nurse in London who decides that from now on, her remittances will go through the Mesh even if it means filling out two extra forms; the Jamaican teacher in Kingston who joins the land trust and spends her Saturday mornings in meetings instead of doom-scrolling; the mechanic in West Philly who buys one co-op share instead of one more pair of shoes he doesn't need; the software engineer in Lagos who accepts a lower salary from an Afro-owned infrastructure co-op instead of a higher one from a multinational that treats his city as a data mine; the retiree in Baltimore who moves her checking account from the mega-bank that left her neighborhood decades ago to the Black credit union that's been holding it down since she was a child.

None of them will ever be on Forbes. But collectively, they are the largest underreported investor class on earth: people who refuse to be only consumers of whatever the old system offers, and quietly become owners of the essentials in their own story.

Epilogue Without Ending

This is the last chapter, but not an ending. Fiction can end neatly. Real life shrugs and says, "To be continued…" Somewhere, even as you read this: a regulation is being drafted that will either help or hinder the next co-op; a stablecoin whitepaper is being written that will either learn from this history or pretend it never happened; a teenager is walking past an empty storefront that will either be a payday lender… or a community-owned clinic… or a "Luxury Wash Experience"… or something nobody has imagined yet.

In that sense, 2029 is not a date. It's a test. Not of central banks. Not of hedge funds. Not of AI. Of us.

Do we still believe the only directions are "up" and "back"? Or will we finally take the third option: "through and across"— through the crash, across to something we own together?

WPBS was always a joke and a prophecy in one line: "The West Philadelphia Billionaires Society." The joke is obvious. The prophecy is this: "Billionaire" doesn't just mean personal net worth. It means a community with assets, dignity, and options so wide that a single market crash cannot erase them. Will there be future crashes? Yes. Systems wobble. Powers shift. Human nature does what human nature does. But by the time the next graph falls off the cliff in some future year's Crash Week, there will be more: Mesh nodes woven, blocks stabilized, co-ops matured, land taken off the auction block and entrusted to people who remember Greenwood and vow not to repeat its fate.

So this is where the book stops talking.

The prophetic part is already done:

- It warned that "post-MAGA" wouldn't mean "post-chaos."
- It showed how "safe-ish" can sink ships.
- It hinted at how laundromats, land, and long-distance love could be the start of a different regime.

What happens next is not on the page. It's on the block. In the budget. In the remittance. In the board meeting. In the prayer. Because if 2029 taught us anything, it's this: Systems fall. Stories fail. But people who are rooted, networked, and awake can walk through the rubble, look at one another, and say, without flinching: "We are still here. We still own something. And by the grace of God, we are not done building yet."

Chapter 13

The Owner's Manual for a Shaky Planet

History likes to pretend it's neat. Things get names like: "The Great Depression." "The Global Financial Crisis." "The 2029 Post-MAGA Crash." Boom. One title. One era. One tidy chapter in a textbook. In real life, it never feels like that. It feels like:

- "The year the laundromat almost closed."
- "The month Grandma's rent went up and her blood pressure went with it."
- "That time you refreshed your account three times because you were sure the app was broken."

What this book has been doing, quietly, is sneaking a different genre into the canon. Not just crisis narrative, but owner's manual. Not for markets. For communities living on a shaky planet. This last chapter is not about another plot twist in 2029. It's about what stubborn, rooted people did next—and what their spreadsheets, deeds, and co-op bylaws were really saying underneath all the numbers.

What Never Went Back to "Normal"

When the dust settled—not all at once, but in those slow-motion years after 2029—certain things simply never snapped back:

1. Blind trust died.
    - "Safe-ish" products never regained their halo.
    - The phrase "capital preservation" stopped sounding like a guarantee and started sounding like a question.

2. The central bank fairy tale shrank.
   - People still expected interventions—but not miracles.
   - The "central bank put" became more conditional, more political, and less comforting.
3. The myth of the passive consumer cracked.
   - It became painfully obvious that households weren't just "end users" of financial products.
   - They were, collectively, the main source of deposits, fees, and flows that kept the system alive.

Meanwhile, something else started to look less like a footnote and more like a headline: Wherever cooperative ownership, community finance, and land stewardship had taken root, the crash landed differently. Researchers and organizers kept tracing the roots back to the same soil:

- Black mutual aid and cooperative traditions in the Americas, built as a response to enslavement, exclusion, and racism—farmers' unions, buying clubs, housing co-ops, credit unions, and mutual insurance societies.
- Worker cooperatives like Mondragón in Spain—a federation of tens of thousands of worker-owners whose top managers earned only several times the lowest salary, with profits reinvested in jobs and community rather than outside shareholders.
- Community land trusts (CLTs)—nonprofits that keep land in community hands and housing permanently affordable by owning the land and leasing it to residents, so it can't be flipped out from under them with each speculative cycle.
- Community Development Financial Institutions (CDFIs)—mission-driven banks, credit unions, loan

funds, and VC funds that exist specifically to serve low-income and underserved communities, backed by the U.S. CDFI Fund to expand lending, affordable housing, and small-business financing.

Different regions. Different histories. Same pattern:

When people shut out of "normal" finance built their own institutions, they accidentally wrote a field manual for surviving the future. WPBS was that manual, written in diaspora dialect and church-basement tone. This chapter just organizes what was already there.

Thirteen WPBS Laws for Living After 2029

Nobody put these on a stone tablet. They came out of: board meetings that ran long, prayer circles that went off-agenda, arguments over whether the laundromat should get new machines or a new roof first. They're not "rules." They're patterns—things that kept showing up wherever communities stayed standing after the ground shook.

Law 1 – Crashes Are Features, Not Bugs

Systems built on leverage, hope, and "past performance" will crash. Not if.

When. Financial historians have documented cycles for centuries; the particular triggers change, but the pattern of boom, overconfidence, fragility, and crash repeats. WPBS people stopped treating crashes as: "black swans," "unthinkable events," or "acts of God."They treated them like winter: unwanted, sometimes brutal, but absolutely part of the climate. And once you accept winter is real, you pack differently.

Law 2 – No Story Is Risk-Free

If a product, platform, or pundit keeps using the word "safe" like seasoning—sprinkled on everything—assume there's something you're not being told. WPBS veterans knew "cash-plus," "market-neutral," "stablecoin," "inflation-protected," are not magic shields. They're design choices and legal documents wearing marketing perfume.

Communities with a tradition of cooperative economics learned this the hard way: if formal markets shut you out or exploit you, you start your own—farmers' cooperatives, mutual aid funds, Black credit unions, and collective land ownership.

The lesson: There is no such thing as risk-free. There is only risk we understand and share, versus risk we outsource and pray about later.

Law 3 – The People Are Already the Capital

By the time 2029 arrived, migrant remittances—those $50, $200, $500 at a time—had quietly grown into a river of hundreds of billions of dollars a year flowing to low- and middle-income countries, outpacing foreign aid and sometimes even foreign investment. For decades, that river had been treated as: a "development variable," a lifeline, somebody else's spreadsheet line.

WPBS flipped the script: Remittances are not pity money. They're not just survival money. They're investment potential—if even a small share is channeled into co-ops, land trusts, and community funds alongside daily needs. Diaspora Mesh nodes didn't invent remittances; they just intercepted 1–5% of what people were already sending and steered it toward shared assets.

The law underneath: The money is already leaving fingers. The only question is whether some of it returns as ownership, not just as receipts.

Law 4 – If It Doesn't Survive a Phone Call, It's Not Community

You can't build a resilient system on anonymous flows alone. When shocks hit, the institutions that held together best had something in common: members knew each other's names, could show up at a meeting, could call somebody when terms needed to flex.

Black cooperatives, credit unions, land trusts, and co-ops historically grew out of relationships—churches, lodges, unions, neighborhoods—where people had to rely on each other because mainstream institutions either shut them out or preyed on them. Mondragón didn't become a global cooperative group by anonymous stock trades; it built systems where workers became members, shared governance, and stayed through cycles.

The law: If nobody can pick up the phone, change a term, or bring soup when somebody's sick, that structure is not your core safety net. Use it. Trade with it. Bless it.

But don't build your peace of mind on it.

Law 5 – Land Is a Theology Decision

Community Land Trusts have a simple, almost rude premise: "Land is too important to be left fully at the mercy of the speculative market." So CLTs hold land in nonprofit entities and lease it out long-term, keeping housing and some commercial spaces permanently affordable while allowing residents to build some equity.

You can argue about policy. You can debate the models. But beneath the legal structures is a spiritual claim:

- "This neighborhood is not a roulette wheel."
- "People are not temporary placeholders for higher-paying tenants."
- "We would rather cap upside than guarantee displacement."

WPBS borrowed that mindset, then added Greenwood's ghost in the room—Tulsa's Black Wall Street, built by Black entrepreneurs and professionals and then destroyed in a 1921 racist massacre whose scale and official complicity scholars and recent public reports have been documenting more fully in the last decade.

The theology of land became: "We refuse to build another Black Wall Street on land somebody else can torch, tax, or take at will." That's not just economics. That's doctrine.

Law 6 – If the Ratio Is 400:1, That's Not a Relationship

In a typical large corporation, the CEO can earn hundreds of times the salary of the lowest-paid worker. Mondragón's worker cooperatives, by contrast, have long kept pay ratios much tighter—research and reporting note that top salaries are generally capped at around six times the lowest, with some exceptions still far below traditional corporate extremes, and profits shared among worker-members. That doesn't make Mondragón heaven on earth. It makes it honest:

- "We're all in this."
- "If you sweat here, you share here."
- "Leadership earns more, but not that much more."

WPBS took the spirit, if not the exact numbers: co-ops where no one could 400x the janitor's pay, community funds where returns were capped for outside capital, governance that kept decision-makers tied to the impact of their decisions.

Law 6 is simple: If the upside is private but the downside is socialized, it's not partnership. It's extraction with snacks.

Law 7 – Don't Call It "Alternative" If It's Keeping You Alive

CDFIs were once dismissed as "alternative finance"—niche, marginal, side-projects. Then crisis after crisis hit, and it turned out these mission-driven lenders were the ones: still making small loans in disinvested areas, financing affordable housing and essential services, reaching borrowers mainstream banks didn't bother with.

Federal reports and oversight bodies now describe CDFIs as central to expanding capital in low-income communities, with billions in lending and investment for small businesses and housing in recent years. The label "alternative" says more about who's doing the labeling than about what's essential.

For a lot of neighborhoods, CDFIs and Black-owned credit unions were the only banks that ever took them seriously.

WPBS law: If it's the only lender who shows up in bad times, it's not "alternative." It's primary infrastructure in disguise.

Law 8 – Scale Is Overrated. Pattern Is Everything.

You can always throw a big number on a slide:

- "81,000 worker-owners in Mondragón."
- "Roughly 160+ community land trusts in the U.S."
- "Billions of dollars lent through CDFIs."

The temptation is to worship scale:

- "We'll be safe when we're that big."
- "We'll be powerful when we have those numbers."

But the WPBS pattern was: one laundromat, one block, one cold-storage co-op, one credit union branch, one remittance circle. The miracle wasn't that any one project dominated a market. The miracle was that the same pattern kept emerging: shared ownership, shared risk, shared upside, land and money pulled just slightly off the casino floor. Scale is nice. Pattern is holy.

Law 9 – The Ledger Is a Liturgical Document

Every budget is a worship service with no music. Look line by line:

- Where does money consistently flow?
- Who gets paid first?
- Who never appears at all?

Historically, Black cooperative experiments, from mutual aid societies to consumer co-ops, tied economics to explicit values—self-help, solidarity, and collective uplift in the face of systemic exclusion. Mondragón bakes education, solidarity funds, and community reinvestment into its structure. Community land trusts legally embed "this land is for community benefit in perpetuity."

WPBS added our own flavor: tithes and offerings alongside co-op dues, emergency funds next to capital expenditures, "community dividends" posted on the same board as profit distributions.

The law: Show me your recurring payments, and I'll show you what you actually believe is sacred.

Law 10 – The Next Crash Is Already Booked. The Next Response Is Not.

Nothing in this book prevents the next big wobble:

- AI models will panic again at the same time.
- Some "new" product will blow up looking suspiciously like an old one in different packaging.
- Some government will pull a San Aurelio and slam down capital controls while pretending everything is fine.

That's baked in. What is not baked in is how many: land trusts, co-ops, CDFI-strengthened institutions, diaspora Mesh streams will be in place before it hits.

The students of Black cooperative history remind us: communities created co-ops and credit unions as defensive strategies, to survive market failure and discrimination.

The next wave can be offensive: not just "keep us alive," but "let us buy the assets they drop," "let us anchor the blocks they flee," "let us own the basics they keep overpricing."

WPBS law: Crashes are scheduled. Prepared responses are optional.

Law 11 – Diaspora Is Not Just Distance. It's Leverage.

For centuries, being scattered—by ships, by economics, by war—meant: missing funerals, missing graduations, missing the land your grandparents left behind. Remittances turned that sorrow into a lifeline. Black cooperatives and mutual aid societies turned that lifeline into institutions. The Mesh turned those institutions into leverage: a nurse in London affecting land tenure in Accra, a bus driver in Philly influencing solar grids in Kingston, a programmer in Lagos writing code that makes diaspora flows cheaper, faster, and more locally controlled.

Diaspora stopped being "far from home." It became: "Present in multiple economies, with receipts in all of them." That's not just sentimental. That's balance-sheet power.

Law 12 – Hope Without Structure Is Just a Nice Song

Every movement has two tracks:

1. The anthem:
    - the sermons,
    - the slogans,
    - the goosebumps.

2. The architecture:
    - bylaws,
    - operating agreements,
    - loan covenants,
    - land deeds.

Black co-ops and mutual aid societies often combined both—singing hymns while drafting constitutions, preaching liberation while filling in membership forms.

Mondragón has a whole ecosystem of education, research, and finance behind its rhetoric of worker ownership. Community land trusts wrap "we're staying" into binding legal structures.

WPBS, at its best, refused to stop at: "Let's be billionaires in our minds." It kept going until there were: signed documents, registered entities, bank accounts, and crisis-tested operations.

The law is obvious: Hope is the engine. Structure is the chassis.A movement without both is just a beautifully painted car up on blocks.

Law 13 – The Billion Is Collective or It Isn't Real

The title—The West Philadelphia Billionaires Society—was always half joke, half prophecy. Yes, there will always be individuals with large personal net worths. But in this story, "billionaire" stopped meaning one person's private hoard. It meant: a community with billions in durable, widely owned assets; a network of land, co-ops, funds, and Mesh flows robust enough that no single crash can erase its dignity or bargaining power.

The history of Black cooperative economics makes one thing brutally clear: whenever wealth tried to centralize in a few hands under hostile regimes, it became an easy target for sabotage and dispossession. Shared structures—co-ops, land trusts, credit unions—didn't just spread benefits. They made it harder to decapitate a community's economic life with one racist riot, one bank failure, or one algorithmic panic.

The last law is less finance, more altar call: If only a handful make it out "rich," and the block, the village, the parish remain disposable, that is not a win.

The billion that matters is: shared enough to defend, rooted enough to outlast elections and fads, holy enough to be held loosely and stewarded fiercely.

A Kid Walking Home in 2040

Picture one more scene. It's 2040-something. A kid—call her Amara—is walking home from school in West Philly. She passes: a laundromat where the workers and some neighbors own the place, a clinic with a waiting room full of languages and a board full of locals, a row of houses where the land is owned by a community trust, a credit union that sponsored her robotics club, a mural of Greenwood, Mondragón, and a diagram of a community land trust that somebody's cousin painted.

Her phone buzzes with: a notification that her auntie in London just sent a remittance through a Mesh-linked credit union; a class chat about their field trip to a solar co-op; a news alert about "heightened market volatility due to algorithmic strategies."

She doesn't panic. Not because the world is safe—it isn't. But because: her block has seen one crash already; her church basement has a history of turning panic into planning; her grandparents can point to specific buildings and say, "We own a piece of that. We almost lost it in '29. We didn't."

To a policymaker, she's a tiny dot in a demographic chart. To a WPBS ledger, she's: future board member, future steward, future signer of the next covenant.

The markets will still wobble. Politicians will still posture. AI will still hallucinate and overcorrect. But Amara will grow up inside a different default: "Of course we own something together. Of course crashes come and go. Of course our people are in Accra, Kingston, Lagos, Toronto, London, Philly… And of course, we budget like we intend to still be here after the next storm."

That quiet "of course" is the real plot twist of this whole book. Not that 2029 crashed.

But that, in the wreckage, enough people looked at each other—nurses, bus drivers, aunties, coders, pastors, elders—and said: "We are not just surviving this story. We are rewriting who owns the set, who controls the lights, and who gets to stay when the cameras leave."

Chapter 14

A Letter Mailed Backwards in Time

If books could misbehave, this one already has. It pretended to be: a market-crash thriller, a prophetic sermon in disguise, a diaspora love letter, a community finance manual, and now, here at the end, it's going to try one more trick: It's going to mail itself backwards in time. Not with a time machine—those are still on backorder. Just with a simple assumption:

Somebody is reading this before their 2029. On a lunch break. On a bus. On a couch, side-eyeing their banking app. And whether they know it or not, they're already living in the prequel.

The View From "After"

From the far side of the 2029 crash, the world did not become utopia. Let's be honest:

- Populism didn't evaporate; it changed outfits.
- AI didn't save us; it added new ways to panic faster.
- The "global order" didn't heal; it fractured into blocs, alliances, and awkward group chats.

But something else became clearer than it had ever been:

1. Crashes were not rare. They were baked into systems that relied on leverage, hype, and wilful amnesia about risk.
2. Communities were not helpless. Wherever people had quietly built:
    - worker cooperatives like Mondragón in Spain, where tens of thousands of worker-owners share control and cap executive pay at a few times the lowest wage;

  - community land trusts that hold land in nonprofit hands and lease it back long-term to keep housing and local assets permanently affordable;
  - community development financial institutions (CDFIs) and mission-driven banks that lend billions into low-income neighborhoods mainstream finance calls "too risky";
  - transnational remittance flows treated not only as survival cash but as patient capital… the crash hit differently. Not softly. Not painlessly. Differently.

3. History refused to stay buried. Investigations and reports finally acknowledged old truths: that in 1921, law enforcement and white mobs systematically destroyed Tulsa's Greenwood—"Black Wall Street"—with killings, arson, and theft, and that the financial damage echoes a century later in home values and Black wealth gaps.

On one screen, you could see the new: tokenized assets, AI risk engines, digital dollars. On another, you could see the old: dispossession, extraction, and the stubborn brilliance of people who refused to die broke and invisible. WPBS lived in the overlap.

How the Book Got Loose

The official story is that 2029: The Post-MAGA Global Financial Market Crash was: drafted by a slightly mischievous, slightly tired preacher-coach who loved Jesus, NLP, spreadsheets, and the African Diaspora, published too early for some people's comfort and too late for others', shelved in "Economics" by algorithms that had no idea what to do with all the altar calls.

The unofficial story is better. In that version, the book kept slipping out of whatever box people put it in:

- A policy analyst bought it "for research" and ended up highlighting the parts about laundromats and aunties instead of the parts about yield curves.
- A seminary student used it for a paper on "Christian Stewardship in Late Capitalism" and got accused of reading sci-fi.
- A young coder in Lagos used it as mood-board material for building cheaper, more cooperative remittance rails, then forgot to close the PDF in front of her whole dev team.

It moved like a rumor: "You should read this; it's ridiculous, but it's… not wrong." By the time 2029 rolled through like a drunk uncle at a family reunion: some readers had already seen a "CashPlus" in their own life; some had already heard whispers about "stablecoins backed by government debt" and "cash-like funds for institutions;" some had already sat in church basements where someone muttered, "We really could do this WPBS thing, you know… if we stopped acting surprised every time the casino catches fire."

The book did not prevent the crash. Let's not give it more credit than it deserves. But it did something more subtle: It gave certain people language, expectations, and receipts before the headlines caught up.

So when the floor shook: they recognized some of the dance moves, they didn't confuse volatility with the end of the world, and they knew where to look for exits—not just in trading apps, but in land records, co-op bylaws, and Mesh group chats.

The Two Kinds of Reader

Seen from "after," there were really only two kinds of readers:

1. The Tourist Reader
    - Enjoyed the story,

- Underlined the spicy quotes,
- Said things like, "Wow, that would be wild if it ever happened,"
- Then went back to betting their whole emotional life on one number at the top of a browser tab.

2. The Time-Traveler Reader
   - Treated the book as a future postcard,
   - Noticed which parts were fiction and which parts were built out of real-world examples—Mondragón, CLTs, CDFIs, Greenwood, remittances that now total around hundreds of billions annually to low- and middle-income countries;
   - Let a quiet thought form in the back of their mind: "If people like us have already done pieces of this, then this is less prophecy and more memory rehearsal."

The tourist reader closed the book and said, "Crazy world, huh?" The time-traveler reader closed the book and felt the strange sensation of recognition, as if they'd just been handed minutes from a meeting that hadn't happened yet, but would. No altar call. No worksheet.

Just a holy, annoying awareness: "Somebody, somewhere, is already treating this like a manual."

What the Manual Actually Says (Between the Lines)

If you strip away the jokes, the acronyms, the AI, the crash plots, the Half-Bailouts and the Mesh memes, this whole project has been whispering a handful of sentences over and over. They sound like this:

- "No one is coming to permanently stabilize your life from the top down."
- "Remittances, church offerings, susu clubs, and side

hustles have already built more capital than most people realize."

- "Co-ops, land trusts, and CDFIs are not utopian experiments; they are historic survival technologies that quietly kept communities alive when Wall Street and City Hall did not."
- "The 1921 destruction of Greenwood was not an unfortunate footnote; it was a demonstration of what happens when Black prosperity meets white supremacy on land Black people don't structurally control."
- "If you are going to build again, you might as well build like you remember."

That's it. That's the manual. Everything else was just props and parables.

The Running Joke Heaven Keeps Making

In heaven's writers' room (go with me for a second), there is a running joke. It goes like this: Humans keep saying: "This time is unprecedented." And the angels keep scrolling through archives of: empires, booms, busts, revolutions, rebuilds, and responding: "Beloved… the fonts are new. The patterns are ancient."

When 2029 hit, pundits said "unprecedented" so many times the word filed a harassment complaint. But in the data—and in the streets—it rhymed with: previous debt crises, previous shadow-finance blow-ups, previous episodes where governments "discovered" that non-bank leverage could feel an awful lot like a bank run without branches.

The new part wasn't the crash. The new part was: how many people had quietly decided to treat crisis not just as disaster but as raw material; how much historical truth about Greenwood and similar atrocities had finally been dragged into official daylight; how much of the Diaspora had started thinking of themselves not only as senders and receivers, but as co-owners of something bigger than any one country's story.

Heaven's joke, if you listen carefully, is this: "The world is wobbling. Again. And yet… the Spirit has receipts. Again."

A Soft Focus on the One Holding the Book

Somewhere right now, there is: a 17-year-old who just learned about the Tulsa massacre on TikTok before their history teacher mentioned it; a 42-year-old wiring money home so often they can do the exchange rate math in their sleep; a 63-year-old who remembers when the last "once in a lifetime" crisis was supposed to be the last one; a 29-year-old working in tech, watching AI trade the market faster than regulators can Google the acronyms.

One of them is holding this book. Maybe not physically. Maybe as a screenshot of a paragraph someone texted and said, "Read this." They don't have a co-op yet. They don't have a land trust board meeting on their calendar. They don't have a grand plan. What they do have is a growing allergy to being only a consumer: of media, of products, of policies, of "solutions" designed in rooms they're never invited into. They may not have the words yet. That's what this whole messy, footnoted, fictional, prophetic project was for: to give them language for what they already feel, and a picture of what others have already done.

This Is Where the Narrator Bows Out

Books love to end with a big flourish. This one is going to end more like a church service where the formal benediction was ten minutes ago but people are still hugging, still talking, still planning in the aisles. There is no grand finale here. Just a simple timeline:

- Before 2029: People built cooperatives, credit unions, and land trusts they didn't think were glamorous enough to make the news.
- During 2029:Systems crashed; headlines screamed; half-bailouts happened; ordinary people in basements made decisions about buying, building, and banking that would never trend on social media.
- After 2029:Some of those boring, un-Instagrammable decisions turned into:
    - jobs that didn't vanish,
    - homes that didn't gentrify out of existence,
    - institutions that kept lending and serving when "too big to fail" looked surprisingly fragile.
- Beyond 2029: Kids grew up thinking it was normal for their community to:
    - own part of the local grid,
    - have a say in what gets built on their block,
    - receive money from cousins overseas and send dividends back in the other direction.

The narrator can't see past your page turn. From here on, the "prophetic" part is over. The remembering part is up to whoever closes this book and walks back into a world where: remittances are still flowing, injustices like Greenwood still echo in wealth gaps and zoning maps, Mondragón-scale experiments still prove that worker power isn't a fantasy; CDFIs and Black credit unions are still out here making "impossible" loans every weekday.

You are somewhere on that map, whether you believe it yet or not. So here, at last, is the soft landing of Chapter 14: No command. No assignment. Just a gentle, stubborn sentence that has been humming underneath every page:

"The crash is not the main character. The owners are." And if this book has done its strange little job, then somewhere in the back of your mind— behind the worry, behind the headlines, behind the account balances— there is a new, slightly dangerous thought sitting quietly: "We might, in fact, be those owners. Not one day. Not if some billionaire saves us. But simply because we decide that the next time the world shakes, our people will be too rooted to uproot."

Afterword

Reading the Future in Reverse

By the time a reader reaches the end of a book like this, something quiet usually settles in.

Not always an answer.

Sometimes just a clearer question.

All the way through these pages there has been a double vision:

- a fictional 2029 crash playing out like a movie,
- and real memories from 2008, 2020, and a dozen personal "Crash Weeks" humming in the background.

For some, this story may have felt like entertainment.

For others, it has read more like déjà vu.

Some readers will close this book and remember:

- the look on a parent's face when retirement savings vanished;
- the feeling of standing in line at an unemployment office;
- the sound of a news anchor saying "unprecedented" while the pattern felt strangely familiar.

Others will remember:

- the grandmother who stretched one check into three miracles;
- the church that quietly paid light bills while politicians argued on TV;
- the cousin who wired money home every month without ever calling himself "a global financial actor."

If those echoes have been loud, the story has done its work.

What This Book Was Really Doing

On the surface, this has been a story about:

- a post-MAGA world misreading what comes next,
- a global crash triggered by the plumbing of money,
- AI traders, shadow banks, and a Half-Bailout.

Underneath, it has been something else:

- a love letter to the African Diaspora,
- a mirror held up to "normal" finance,
- a set of parables about laundromats, land, and long-distance money.

Certain threads kept weaving through:

<u>Ownership vs. spectatorship</u> – the idea that the crash is not the main character; the owners are.

<u>Memory vs. amnesia</u> – the insistence that Greenwood, redlining, and past crashes are not just trivia; they are part of the operating system.

<u>Community vs. isolation</u> – the picture of basements, barbershops, WhatsApp groups, choir lofts, and kitchen tables as financial planning rooms, whether they admit it or not.

<u>Faith vs. fantasy</u> – the difference between "God will rescue me from every bad decision" and "God will sit with me while I learn to steward what I have in the middle of a shaky planet."

The fiction let the volume be turned up.

The real-world models gave it teeth.

The Real Plot Twist

The great joke woven through this whole project is simple:

Most people assume the main character is:

- the market,
- the crash,
- the president,
- the central bank,
- the newest coin or the latest algorithm.

The whole time, the story has been pointing at someone else.

The real plot twist is the ordinary investor who never calls themselves one:

- the nurse who joins a credit union and a co-op instead of staying in the same old extractive loops;
- the retired teacher who sits on a land trust board instead of just complaining about gentrification;
- the auntie who sends remittances and also sees the possibility of a shared pot for something bigger;
- the bus driver who owns one share of a neighborhood business and suddenly realizes a board meeting is also a prayer meeting in disguise.

None of this guarantees safety. The world is still wild. But it does shift the role: from victim of cycles to steward in cycles; from background character to someone whose decisions quietly redraw the map.

That has always been the heart of WPBS: Not one hero on a magazine cover, but a million "ordinary" people with extraordinary receipts and rooted ownership.

If Any of This Felt Like Your Reflection

For some readers, the most unsettling feeling will not be fear; it will be recognition.

Certain phrases, patterns, and scenes will land like:

> "This sounds too much like my block,"
>
> "...too much like my family,"
>
> "...too much like what my spirit has been whispering and I didn't have language for."

In that moment, the book stops being just a story and starts feeling like a conversation that was already playing in the background of the mind.

There is no assignment hidden here. No secret command.

Only an observation:

Wherever people begin to see themselves not just as consumers, clients, or cases—but as owners, stewards, and co-authors — the future of that neighborhood, that congregation, that village, that diaspora line changes shape.

Whether that happens in West Philadelphia, Kingston, Accra, Lagos, Toronto, London, Baltimore, or some place not named in these pages is beyond the reach of a single book.

But one thing remains true:

The crash is never the last word.

The last word belongs to the people still standing, still breathing, still building, still believing God in the middle of the rubble.

If these pages have, in any way, helped name that reality, then their mission is already complete—even as the real work continues off the page.

READER'S GUIDE

Discussion Questions for Book Clubs, Churches, and Masterminds

Use these questions in a living room, church basement, Zoom circle, barbershop, or diaspora WhatsApp group. No pressure—let the conversation breathe.

1. The Crash as Character

   In this story, the 2029 crash feels almost like a character with moods and phases (Hairline Cracks, Crash Week, the Half-Bailout, the long hangover).

   - How did that framing change the way you think about real financial crises you've lived through (2008, 2020, etc.)?
   - Did you notice any parallels? Where did it feel too real?

2. Trust, or the Lack Thereof

   A major theme is collapsing trust—in institutions, markets, and "grown-ups with microphones."

   - Which scene or chapter captured that distrust most powerfully for you?
   - Where do you see this same dynamic in the real world today?

3. WPBS: Vision or Delusion?

   At first, "West Philadelphia Billionaires Society" sounds like a joke. Over time it becomes a serious blueprint.

- At what point in the book did WPBS start feeling plausible to you?
- Which parts of the WPBS model (buy/build/bank, laundromats, land trusts, credit unions, Mesh) feel most realistic? Which feel hardest to imagine actually happening?

4. Winners, Losers, and "Prepared People"

The story is clear: not everyone wins in 2029. But "victory" is defined differently for WPBS investors.

- How does this novel redefine winning and losing in a crisis?
- Do you agree with that definition? Why or why not?

5. The Diaspora Mesh

We see diaspora money (remittances) reframed from survival cash into collective leverage.

- How has the book changed your view of "sending money home"?
- What emotions come up when you think about diaspora as power, not just distance?

6. Fiction vs. Prophecy

The author keeps saying, "This is fiction, but not fantasy."

- Which elements felt frighteningly believable?
- Did any part feel too far-fetched… or not far enough?

7. Role of Faith and Church Basements

Throughout the novel, faith shows up in budgets, bylaws, and board meetings—not just in sermons.

- How did you feel about the way Scripture, prayer, and church life were woven into economic decisions?
- Does your faith community (if you have one) talk this concretely about money, ownership, and crises?

8. Ownership vs. Consumption

The book hammers the idea that the crash is not the main character—the owners are.

- What does ownership mean to you after reading this? Land? Shares? Skills? Relationships?
- In your own life, where do you feel more like a consumer than an owner?

9. The Greenwood Shadow

References to Tulsa's Greenwood ("Black Wall Street") and other historical wounds hang over the story.

- How did those echoes of history affect the way you read the chapters about land trusts and shared ownership?
- Did it make you more hopeful, more wary, or both?

10. Your Crash Week

Everyone has a metaphorical "Crash Week"—a medical crisis, job loss, divorce, war, or financial shock.

- If you're comfortable sharing: what was yours?
- Looking back, what did you wish existed in your community that didn't (co-ops, land trusts, credit unions, mutual aid, etc.)?

11. The Ending: Satisfied or Provoked?

At the end, the narrator steps back and insists: "The crash is not the main character. The owners are."

- Did the ending leave you feeling hopeful, angry, activated, or something else?
- If there were a sequel set 10–15 years later, what would you want to see in that world?

FROM FICTION TO BLUEPRINT

Real-World Inspirations Behind the Story

Although the characters, countries, and coins in this book are fictional, many of the models are lifted from real life. Use this as a cheat sheet.

Note: This is a story, not formal research—but these concepts exist in the real world and are worth exploring.

Worker Cooperatives (Mondragón & Beyond)

The idea of businesses owned and governed by their workers is not fantasy. Worker co-ops—from local bakeries to the Mondragón Cooperative Corporation in Spain—have existed for decades and, in some cases, employ tens of thousands of worker-owners.

In the book: WPBS laundromats and essential services start moving toward shared ownership, profit-sharing, and worker voice.

Community Land Trusts (CLTs)

CLTs are nonprofits that own land and lease it long-term to residents or businesses, with rules that keep housing and local space permanently affordable and rooted in the community. They exist in cities, towns, and rural areas across the U.S. and beyond.

In the book: The "Don't Sell Grandma's House" chapter and the mini-CLT around abandoned lots and rowhouses are built on these models.

Community Development Financial Institutions (CDFIs) & Credit Unions

CDFIs, Black-owned banks, and community credit unions are mission-driven financial institutions that lend and bank in neighborhoods that big banks often ignore or exploit. In reality, they have financed billions in small-business loans, affordable housing, and community projects.

In the book: The "little fund that saw people, not risk" and the Mesh-connected credit unions are rooted in this tradition.

Black Cooperative & Mutual Aid Traditions

From the 1800s through Jim Crow and the Civil Rights era, Black communities used cooperatives, mutual aid societies, savings clubs, insurance funds, and Black-owned banks to survive exclusion, economic violence, and racism.

In the book: WPBS is a modern remix of those traditions, filtered through 21st-century technology and global Diaspora connections.

Greenwood / "Black Wall Street"

The 1921 Tulsa massacre, where a thriving Black business district was destroyed by racist violence and government complicity, is tragically real. Its financial impact still echoes in Black wealth gaps and land ownership patterns.

In the book: Greenwood's ghost walks quietly behind every conversation about land, speculation, and "we will not build prosperity on land we do not structurally control."

Remittances & the Diaspora Mesh

Remittances—money sent by migrants back home—now total hundreds of billions of dollars a year worldwide, often surpassing foreign aid for many countries. Families use them for food, housing, education, healthcare, and small businesses.

In the book: The "Diaspora Mesh" imagines what happens when 1–5% of these flows—just the piece usually eaten by fees or impulse—are redirected into cooperatives, land trusts, community infrastructure, and credit unions.

This novel weaves all of these into a what-if:

What if communities, especially the African Diaspora, took these existing tools seriously before the next crash, and treated them not as exotic experiments, but as core survival technologies?

IF THIS BOOK STIRRED YOU...

Gentle Next Steps (No Hype, Just Possibilities)

This is not financial advice. This is a menu of possibilities, not a command.

If something in these pages woke up a question or a deep "hmm," here are a few gentle directions you might explore in your own time, with your own trusted advisors and community:

1. Learn the Names of Your Local "WPBS-Type" Institutions
    - Is there a Black-owned bank, credit union, CDFI, or community bank near you (or online) that serves your community?
    - Is there a housing co-op, land trust, or worker-owned business in your city?

    Just knowing they exist changes how you see your options.

2. Have One Honest Conversation with Your People

    Not a "let's start a billion-dollar fund by Friday" talk. Just:

    - "What happened to you in 2008 / 2020 / your personal Crash Week?"
    - "What did we wish existed?"
    - "Do co-ops, land trusts, or credit unions already exist near us?"

3. Pick One Model to Study, Not All of Them
    - Worker co-ops
    - Land trusts

- Credit unions / CDFIs
- Diaspora investment clubs / savings circles

Go deep on one. Learn the language and real-life examples. See how people have done this already, not just in theory.

4. Audit Your Own "Ownership vs. Consumption" Mix

   Quietly ask yourself:

   - How much of my monthly life is pure consumption?
   - How much builds any kind of stake—no matter how small—in something real (land, skills, relationships, co-ops, community institutions)?

5. Bring Your Faith (If You're a Believer) into the Money Conversation

   - Pray over your budget.
   - Ask: "Where is fear driving me? Where is fantasy driving me? Where is stewardship calling me?"
   - Consider how Scripture on justice, jubilee, debt, and stewardship might shape not just your giving, but your ownership patterns.

6. Support the People Already Doing the "Boring" Work

   There are already people in your city filling out the paperwork, fighting with zoning boards, writing grant proposals, explaining co-ops to confused bankers, and holding community meetings that 12 people show up to.

   - Maybe your role is to join them.
   - Maybe your role is to pray for them, fund them, or simply not quit your own post.

Again: this is a novel, not a manual. But if it nudged you from spectator toward steward, then it has done its strange little job.

MORE

FROM AARON M. MONTAGUE & MX3

If this story spoke to you, you may also enjoy Aaron's other works that orbit the same universe of faith, identity, money, and community:

Books & Devotionals

MONEY MOVES: Waking Up Your Inner Billionaire Citizen (WPBS Edition)

A practical, faith-filled guide to renewing your mind about money, moving from victim to steward, and aligning your finances with Kingdom purpose and community power.

THE WEST PHILADELPHIA BILLIONAIRES SOCIETY: A Blueprint for Community-Owned Wealth and Prosperity

The orignal "sister" to this novel—laying out the WPBS model in detail: buy, build, bank; governance, training, dividends; and the eight "mountains of influence" for community-owned enterprise.

THE MIRROR: When Your Reflection Starts Talking Back to You

A richly metaphorical, hypnotic journey into identity, self-talk, trauma, and transformation—written like a conversation with your own reflection and the God who placed His image in you.

31 DAYS OF WISDOM: Meditative Prayers from Proverbs

Daily prayers, reflections, and testimonies inspired by the Book of Proverbs, with contributions and stories from family and friends. Designed to speak to both the conscious and subconscious mind with Scripture, affirmation, and gentle inner work.

NOT WHO WE ARE

A piercing, prophetic commentary on language, identity, and national character—confronting how words, labels, and systems have told us a false story about who we are, and inviting readers into repentance, reclamation, and a truer, Kingdom-centered sense of self and community.

If your heart is stirred to move from "reading the story" to "understanding the blueprint," explore more of Aaron's work, teachings, and upcoming projects wherever MX3 content is shared. See https://mx3mtivationalbooks.com for an up-to date list of books, commentaries and blog posts.

2029

About the Author

Aaron Maxwell Montgaue

Aaron M. Montague, MBA, MDiv, PNLP, PTT, CCHt, CSC is a retired U.S. Armed Forces veteran, pastor, financial disciple of Jesus Christ, and hypnotic-trance therapist. Through Montague Motivational Ministries (MX3) and the West Philadelphia Billionaires Society (WPBS) vision, he helps believers move from fear and confusion about money to bold, community-centered stewardship.

He is the author of:

- Money Moves: Waking Up Your Inner Billionaire Citizen (WPBS Edition)
- The West Philadelphia Billionaires Society: A Blueprint for Community-Owned Wealth and Prosperity
- The Mirror: When Your Reflection Starts Talking Back to You
- 31 Days of Wisdom: Meditative Prayers from Proverbs
- Not Who We Are

And more

In 2029: The Post-MAGA Global Financial Market Crash, Aaron blends Scripture, economic insight, humor, and prophetic imagination to offer not just a warning about the next crash, but a vision of communities too rooted to uproot.

www.ingramcontent.com/pod-product-compliance
Lightning Source LLC
Chambersburg PA
CBHW041259210926
51847CB00009B/74
9781967006359